The Best You

Mohammed Haroon

III Clink
Street

London | New York

Published by Clink Street Publishing 2016

Copyright © 2016

First edition.

ISBN: 978-1-911110-46-0
eBook ISBN: 978-1-911110-47-7

This book is dedicated to my children

Kashif, Saba-ul-Ann, Jahanzeabe, Mamoon Zain

And my beloved wife Shamim Haroon

Contents

Preface

All religions and philosophies have a basic understanding that there is one creator or source – whether we call this creative force *God, Nature, the Universe, Consciousness, Vibration, the Matrix, the Field* – from where all knowledge flows.

Human beings have the most powerful brains among all living things on this planet. We have the power to create our own reality. The ultimate power of creation lies with the Creator. We are but a reflection of the Creator. In other words, we are co-creators: i.e. we create together with the help or guidance of the Creator.

We humans have created, are creating, and will be creating everything with our thoughts, which becomes a kind of meditation. There are as many forms of meditation as there are co-creators and they all use some sort of meditation to fulfill their prayers: their wishes, desires for anything they want – health, wealth, solutions to their problems.

To know our own true self, we must be aware of the crucial role played by our *brain, conscious, subconscious* and *unconscious* aspects of our mind and the *heart*. First of all, however, it is essential to know who we are, why we are here and what the real purpose of our life is.

Knowledge is power. My journey into this empowering self-awareness began for me from an early age. I was a restless and inquisitive child, always searching for something strange, unique and wonderful. I never knew why I was so curious but I was very interested in mysticism and miracles and always wanted to know how and why such things exist.

By the age of 16, I enjoyed going to the nearby woods and gorges and sitting motionless in complete silence for hours in the tranquil surroundings. I still remember the night of meditation for enlightenment and bliss that transformed my whole life and caused a paradigm shift in my thinking. I suddenly felt so uplifted and serene, as if all my questions were plainly answered in one flash of wisdom, as I realised 'you have everything you ever need to know, be the thing, and see the thing you want, just know yourself'.

That's when, I began to discover the truth in the most unexpected places. As I progressed in my quest, it dawned on me that it was in fact the power of my questions that led me to the right people, places or events for the right answers. An attempt is made to explain, to the best of my knowledge, about the mysterious power of asking the right question in Chapter 17.

In this book, I want to share my opinions based upon my experiences and studies. I realised that 80% of the information on any subject is easily available through books, magazines, newspapers, lectures, online or through mentoring. In the West, thinkers, philosophers and motivators are more liberal in sharing their thoughts, but keep a small percentage of 'key knowledge or secrets' in their chests or hearts (an oriental concept) for ulterior motives. Perhaps, they do so, for example, to accumulate more wealth or political power. In the East, on the other hand, one has to be far more careful, especially in regard to religion and belief. Therefore, in the East, enlightened persons keep their knowledge buried in their chests and only very serious seekers get closer to this knowledge. The 'chest knowledge' analogy is a quite familiar concept among eastern thinkers and comes from the Arabic word *sadar*.

As the first small step towards improving your life, I ask you to try out the ideas (the ones you agree with) presented in this book. If you find anything of value in this book, or it helps you in any way, by all means pass it on to those whom you care about and for whom you wish greater success. My goal is to make a difference for as many people as possible, but to do this I need your help.

Remember the words of Albert Schweitzer, French philosopher and physician: 'Wherever you turn, you can find someone who needs you. Even if it is a little thing, do something for which there is no pay but the privilege of doing it. Remember, you don't live in a world all of your own.'

That's why to help the poor and needy children in rural Kashmir, I founded the Uspar Trust, a UK registered charitable organisation in 2006. By the end of December 2015 my charity completed several health and education projects, which are fully explained on our website: www.uspar.org.uk.

Therefore, my own personal motto is that we gain the greatest sense of satisfaction in life by helping others. It is also the reason why I have written this book.

Introduction

To make ourselves understand how important we really are, we need to invest in ourselves and treat ourselves like an honoured guest.

How much we achieve in life depends to a huge degree on how well we can communicate with our inner self. Knowing ourselves differs from merely thinking about ourselves. As soon as we fully know ourselves, then we acquire a level of understanding which goes beyond words.

'Knowing yourself is the beginning of all wisdom.' – Aristotle, Ancient Greek philosopher and scientist.

Khalil Gibran, the famous artist, poet, and writer, explains this vital concept in greater detail: 'Knowledge of the self is the mother of all knowledge. So it is up to me to know myself, to know it completely, to know its details, its characteristics, its subtleties, and its very atoms.'

Our true self is hidden under many layers of different personality traits, like the skins of an onion. These layers we acquire, consciously or unconsciously, as we get older. The more we try to get rid of these layers of the ego, the more we discover our true self and this in turn allows us to know who we really are and what we want to achieve in life.

We all earnestly seek the 'Truth' and explore every avenue towards it. Everything we see around ourselves is created by human beings. It exists as a thought in the human mind. A thought is creative; whatever we desire always begins as a thought. So everything is created twice, firstly in the mind by the imagination and secondly in reality.

Nature compels us all to move through life, to strive, to improve, to achieve. All this necessarily entails continual mental development. We cannot remain still, however much we may desire to do so. This development can occur only through improving the quality of our thoughts. Studying the creative process of our thoughts and how to apply them is of supreme importance to each one of us. This knowledge is the means whereby the evolution of human life on earth may be accelerated and elevated.

Just think: if our life is simply a function of our own personal creation, and like a designer we can reshape our life, then imagine what wonderful things we can achieve!

Everything in the universe is within us. Everyone has brief moments or 'flashes of success'. **Whatever we're looking for can only be found inside of us.** There is a reality architect or a higher inspiring co-creator within us and all we need to do is become aware of that. Whenever we try to improve anything, this always means in the first place that there is something wrong. For example, if we wish to become wealthier, this therefore signifies that we don't have enough money.

There is already a perfect reality here. This reality is invisible and even intangible right now, but is also substantial and real. Our reality is more real than the chair we are sitting on because it is unchangeable and cannot be diminished or destroyed.

Our true inner self is complete and perfect; it lies dormant. Once awake, it shows its true worth. We see this in the life of Michelangelo, the famous Italian sculptor. He was born with this gift of perception. He showed no interest in his schooling, preferring to copy paintings from churches and seek the company of painters. Therefore, by the time he had finished his artistic apprenticeship, he understood that he could not just turn a block of marble into a work of genius with his chisel and hammer but, as he put it, he had to *free* that masterpiece, by envisioning what was hidden inside. As B.C. Forbes, author and financial journalist, puts it, 'Think not of yourself as the architect of your career but as the sculptor. Expect to have to do a lot of hard hammering and chiselling and scraping and polishing.'

The self has everything; all it needs is to fulfil its higher purpose. The same concept is wonderfully put by Rumi, a poet, Islamic scholar, and Sufi mystic: 'You wander from room to room hunting for the diamond necklace that is already around your neck!'

When we desire something, like 'I want to see who I really am from the Creator's perspective; I want to wake up to what is really here in reality', our level of perception will dramatically improve and a real transformation in our prospects will occur. This will immediately give us a glimpse of a far brighter future.

'Set your sights high, the higher the better. Expect the most wonderful things to happen, not in the future but right now. Realise that nothing is too good. Allow absolutely nothing to hamper you or hold you up in any way.' – Eileen Caddy, a spiritual teacher.

There is no such thing as a 'secret formula' or a 'secret behind the secrets', magical or missing ingredients, cutting edge tools, all-purpose manuals or programmes. All this is merely hype, selling false dreams, hoodwinking victims by playing on their emotions.

To achieve our own dreams, we must understand the following two fundamental facts:

1. We must take responsibility, follow our chosen plan and take action.

2. Simply waiting for something good to happen, somehow to be lucky all of a sudden, is merely a waste of time. Nothing can be achieved by being so passive. Within us, there must be a real desire, a determined focus on all our goals.

Do we need long lists of statements, repeating them for hours or listening to a never-ending series of tapes, CDs or MP3s? They may be offered at heavily discounted prices with extra bonuses, but it's all too easy to end up feeling frustrated when things don't change. The choice is ours.

PART ONE

Find the Hidden Vision

1
Our Reality

I'd like to start by saying I may seem at times a little direct but please rest assured that my intended audience is not people in general but rather every unique, fascinating individual who desires the truth. So – dearest individual – let me open with this: We are wonderful, and our life has value and meaning and it too is wonderful. We are a volume in the divine book; a mirror to the power that created the universe.

'You were born with wings, why prefer to crawl through life?' – Rumi, Islamic scholar, and sufi mystic.

'No man can reveal to you aught but that which already lies half-asleep in the dawning of your knowledge.' – Khalil Gibran, artist, poet, and writer.

We are invisible beings living in visible bodies – a physical extension of that which is non-physical. 'We are not human beings having a spiritual experience. We are spiritual beings having a human experience.' Pierre Teilhard de Chardin – French philosopher. We are not only made of body and mind but also the spirit of who we are and what we want to become. It is a mortal body, and an eternal being is dwelling in it. This immortal part of us needs to be uncovered by removing the layers of ego to seek our true self.

On the spiritual level, we all are equal because we share the same divine source, but, on the non-spiritual level, we are different because of the egotism of our earthly life. We can recognise this in the way people think: 'What's in it for me? How can I get more? I want a BMW in my driveway next Thursday.' All of that is what most spiritual teachers call the false self, the ego.

We are not only our thoughts, mind, feelings or body, but also we have limitless capabilities. We have access to anything and everything we wish to have. We are a unique and beautiful expression of the mysterious gift of life and creation. The basis of our life is freedom. According to the Universal Declaration of Human Rights, all human beings are born free and equal in dignity and rights. Our true purpose is to become our own unique self and fundamentally change our own life for the better, and also to help others make a more positive contribution to the world. Life is a journey but not a destination. It is a process full of energy; simply learn to enjoy it as we go along. We are co-creators; we create with our every thought.

When we begin to work with our inner or true self, we start to exercise higher levels of free will. Free will provides the general direction we want to go in, but not the actual means to get there. Relax and learn to go with the flow, even if not everything may turn out as we wish. We may be guided to a better alternative because the Creator knows better for us. Our true self is always in alignment with what is best for us. Once we act in accordance with our true self, it is impossible to be lonely or desperate. Connecting with and knowing our true self is a life-changing event. This is because we are then emotionally aware of our true self. We will be experiencing the actions, sensations and feelings that go with living a full life. It's wonderful to be associated with such magical moments, moments of great joy and love.

We are made of the same energy as the comets, planets and stars. We are all one, but at the same time separate and individual. That is to say, that we were all created by the same divine force and so are still connected with one another, even though we grow and develop in our unique fashion. What is this energy called? It is known by various names: *Spirit, God, Universe, Creator, Matrix* or *The Field* – invisible forces that influence the physical world. We are all part of that invisible *Universe* or *God*. This force works in 'real time', i.e. instantaneously. It recognises and understands our non-verbal language, which consists of emotion and beliefs.

If we say, 'I would like a perfect partner to appear in twenty minutes from now,' this energy does not acknowledge any concept of time, such as 'twenty minutes from now'. It is a real time application i.e. its actions take place instantaneously. This is why it is absolutely necessary to be specific about what it is we are choosing. What we are trying to do, in this world of infinite possibilities, is to identify and focus on one thought at a time. If we are not specific about what we desire, then how can the universe give us what we desire?

Everything in the universe is made up of easily changeable energy. It's constantly moving, flowing, being pulled in one direction and then another. This affects everything that exists in our life. Energy started as a non-physical form, before changing into a physical form. We have been given creative faculties, unlike any other animal. We are the highest form of creation on the planet. This allows us to have the power of imagination. In turn this means, as we are a part of the same energy as the universe, we are quite capable of using the energy around ourselves to help change our life, according to our own will.

We have the ability to feel in our body the force that holds this universe together. If one particle of matter is split into two and each part is separated physically miles away, still they would be connected energetically. So if one particle were disturbed, the other particle would react the same way. For example, a mother will instinctively know when her child is in danger, even though he may be many miles away.

It is already perfected

Who and what we really are, is already perfected by the Creator. We don't need to improve; we can't improve. Our deepest and most truthful self does not care about trends, struggles, losses or worries. Our true self is free from the world's petty, artificial demands, judgements and expectations. Everything we are, or will ever become, is already part of our true self. It is also true that most people do not know how to make the most of their incredible potential because they do not understand their true self. This is where putting into practice the information contained in this book can open the door to self-discovery and personal growth.

We will discover that everything we have been searching for is within us already. We might have wanted to achieve more but we didn't know how. We might have had no true success, when we were desperate to succeed. We could be just a few stepping stones away from a wonderful life. Perhaps all we need to be is more confident. It may be we can start with thinking more positively and smiling more often. Feeling confident is definitely a continuous process that, when achieved, will improve our quality of life immensely. Be conscious of the fact that we are a miracle. Know how magnificent we are. We are a marvel. We can do something that causes wonder, admiration and astonishment. The examples of man's miracles are countless: the advances in medicine, space travel and atomic energy are just a few we could mention.

Getting rid of the notion of self-improvement is the key. The teachings of the self-improvement gurus are based on the idea that there is something missing or wrong with us which has to be remedied. When we try to make up for something lacking, all we will do is replace one failing with another. The power is already within us. As Michelangelo said, the Creator already created the sculpture and his job was to bring out the vision of that masterpiece already hidden in that block of stone and set it free – or as he put it, 'I let him out.' Everything is here; the world is already created, but it is infinite, forever unfolding.

'We cannot teach people anything; we can only help them discover it within themselves' – Galileo Galilei, astronomer, physicist and philosopher who played a major role in the scientific revolution during the Renaissance.

So our job is to tap into the vision of what is already hidden in this mortal body, this masterpiece, this divine pattern, this potential, and then set it free by creating the right conditions for it to materialise.

When we desire or pray for something more in life, that potential begins to appear instantly. It is only the limitations of our ego which hinder our success.

Very few human beings realise the latent potential they have to alter their own lives. Blindly, they complain about outside forces, such as debt, bad relationships or a lack of opportunity, while remaining unaware of the power they already possess, the power that can alter their current reality.

All the powers in the universe are already ours. It is we who cover our eyes with our own hands and then cry that it is dark. We are what our thoughts have made us; so take care of what we think. Words are secondary. Thoughts live and travel far. When an idea exclusively occupies the mind, it is transformed into an actual physical or mental state.

We have no idea how magnificent we have become. We don't know how brilliant we are, how resourceful, how creative, how worthy we are. Listen to ourselves: we are our own guru. Let's look for the answers in ourselves, not anywhere else. We exist inside one big universe; humans are like individual grains of sand in a never-ending desert. But while we are so tiny, we also possess the power to control our life and pull more of what we do want towards ourselves – and push what we don't want away.

We are made perfect, in the image of the Creator. The more we understand this image, the better it will be. We will then know that we are miraculous. When we acknowledge this, in ourselves and everyone else, then it transforms us and everyone else as well. This is a gift given to everyone.

We reap what we sow; we are the makers of our own fate. No one else is to blame. There is no help for us outside of ourselves. We are the architects of our own reality. We have unquestionable and supreme authority over ourselves. Like the silk worm, we have built a cocoon around ourselves. Liberate ourselves from this cocoon. Be free! Then, and then alone, we will see the truth.

Remember!

We are magnificent individuals and our life is worth living.

Our true objective is transforming our life for the better and also helping others.

Know our true self. This is always best for us.

Rediscover our dreams.

The power of our thoughts can guide us to an exemplary life.

2
Why Are We Here?

'Only a life lived for others is a life worthwhile.'
– Albert Einstein, physicist.

We live for one another. We are social animals, absolutely dependent on each other. Indeed this is the basis of our very survival. After all, think about how a baby needs its parents. Similarly, we have ten thousand billion germs living in harmony inside our body, and without them we would be dead.

Caring for others is an integral part of living; indeed it is what makes life worth living. In other words, caring for others is the art of living. Helping other people, influencing their lives for the better, so that all human life is valued from one generation to the next, gives us the greatest sense of personal achievement possible. Therefore we need to ask ourselves how we can care for others every single day. Accumulating wealth doesn't make us happy. We will always want more. To be happy, give! The art of giving is an essential part of the art of living.

We should all help one another. We should all be able to see the absolute need for us all to be charitable in life. Obviously, everybody can't be like Bill Gates, giving away billions. We probably cannot afford to give away vast amounts of money. That doesn't matter. Indeed, the greatest charity in life is not giving money, food or blood. Sometimes, of greater benefit to society is simply to spare someone else our negative comments. Knowing when it is better not to criticise is another essential element to the true art of living. Judging others negatively often simply causes pain. In this particular context, we arrive at a striking contradiction. This act of charity entails not giving anything; that is to say, passing judgement on others.

Living for the benefit of others helps us all deal with the challenges of life. We are at our happiest when we most want to give to others. Of course, the charitable act may consist of giving time, donating money, helping or simply listening.

> 'One of the secrets of the life is that all that is really worth the doing is what we do for others.' – Lewis Carroll – writer, mathematician and logician.

However, remember, serving others is the greatest act of generosity possible and when one satisfies the need of others even before their asking, that is the act of giving in the truest sense imaginable.

Indeed, nature makes us help one another. It has been demonstrated that being altruistic literally boosts the body's immune system. On the other hand, when we try to harm others, the same immune system is damaged. Therefore, it is possible to say, being cruel to others is literally unhealthy.

At the same time, we should recognise how little we control our lives. Probably only about 15% of what happens to us does so because of the decisions we make. (In truth, if we had total control of our lives, we would not know what to do.) After all, no one asks to be born. Nor can we decide when our lives will reach their natural end. Therefore, some 85% of who we are and what we do comes from our DNA: e.g. our bodily appearance, our physical potential and natural abilities and even arguably, to a limited degree, behaviour and character. For instance, only a very small minority of people have sufficient natural talent to become a professional sportsperson. In addition, I do, however, believe, in essence, in free will. We can make many important decisions for ourselves because our consciousness is a gift from the Creator.

Many books and courses are trying to improve the 15% part of human life. By knowing our true self, once we follow simple ideas presented in the various chapters of this book, we can genuinely improve the remaining 85% control of our life which runs unconsciously. We don't know what is good for us until we are connected with our higher self or consciousness – as is explained in Chapter 6. Once we are allied with our consciousness, things start happening to us automatically. It is like an assistant who sorts everything out for us all the time. True fulfilment comes by tapping into that source of pure essence.

Having a vision of our expectations and hopes is perhaps the best definition of having a true sense of purpose in life. The infinite is the author of our purpose in life. Our greater purpose is already written in the fabric of our being, waiting to be fulfilled. All our expectations are based on hope. Without hope we can expect and know nothing. Hope is also the knowledge that even in the worst of times we can triumph over hardship and sorrow and grow in spirit. Hope meets us halfway on a bridge called faith.

'The wings of hope carry us, soaring high above the driving winds of life.' – Ana Jacob – novelist.

Life is supposed to be enjoyed. Without hope, we cannot feel good nor have fun. See also Chapter 16.

Remember!

All successful people know the art of living. Far from being greedy, they are motivated by a desire to help others.

Meet the challenges that life throws at us with courage.

Life is to be lived with a spirit of hope and achievement. Inspire ourselves.

Avoid passing judgement too readily. Instead of judging people on how they look or for what they have done, try instead to understand them. Put ourselves in their shoes.

PART TWO

Five Powerful Performers

3
The Human Brain

We have two brains – one in our skull and the other in our belly.

The First Brain (in our skull)

'It is a fabulous instrument, the brain.' – Dr Glenn Doman, author and founder of The Institute for the Achievement of Human Potential.

Our brain is a biological supercomputer.
'The human brain has 100 billion neurons, each neuron connected to 10 thousand other neurons. Sitting on our shoulders is the most complicated object in the known universe.' – Michio Kaku, a physicist and populariser of science.

It is designed to achieve goals – any goals (good or bad). Our brain does not think or worry about the end result. It is always **asking questions and looking for the answers** to those questions. It simply helps the owner to achieve whatever he or she is really imagining to achieve through a thought process of asking and searching for the answers.

'The human brain, then, is the most complicated organisation of matter that we know.' – Isaac Asimov, author.

Our brain springs into action whenever we have serious goals or emotion-driven thoughts. Thinking repeatedly about something we really want, we imagine enjoying its benefits. This has an emotional impact. So be careful what we constantly think about or imagine, as the brain is designed to make such dominant thoughts and feelings come true automatically.

If we think a particular skill or set of studies will be difficult, our brain makes this come true. It does so by reducing the level of mental activity during the process. On the other hand, failure is not inevitable. We can get rid of all those unwanted negative expectations by thinking positively. Our brain's *Reticular Activating System* (RAS) acts like a radar detector, helping us keep our goals in mind. It is the gateway through which nearly all information enters our brain. It filters all of this and affects what we pay attention to. Even when we don't realise we're thinking about these goals, our brain knows that they're important and makes note of anything that might relate to them. We will notice anything new and different. At the same time, we can re-train our brain to believe in ourselves, even if we have always felt it's already 'too late'.

There are two hemispheres in the brain. The left side deals with logic, ego and language and controls the right side of the body. The right side is intuitive, almost always 'reading' our surroundings. It is the part of us which expresses our imagination and emotions, that which gives us our sense of consciousness. It also controls the left side of the body.

Our brain is so powerful it transmits and receives signals faster than radio waves. In fact, every cell in a human body emits a different energy or frequency. Indeed, everything on the planet emits vibrations in gaseous form but not as a signal. This energy passes through everything. Whatever frequency our brain transmits, that same is drawn to us magnetically. In other words: what we think, we become.

We have the power in our brain that is far greater than anything we might have to face. It is our free choice over what we want to think. And these are the very thoughts that can make us choose our own destiny. We have the power and ability to create any frequency with our brain and transmit it at any level we want. It is picked up across the globe with the same power.

Our brain is 'plastic' in nature, can indeed physically change. This is called 'brain plasticity' or neuron-plasticity. It refers to the brain's ability to change and adapt as a result of experience. This neuron-plasticity of the brain is the basis of all learning. Until the 1960s, researchers believed that changes in the brain could only take place during infancy and childhood. By early adulthood, the brain's physical structure was thought to be permanent. We now know that this concept is wrong.

Just like there are tissue changes in muscle after exercise, the brain makes changes after brain training as well. It learns new information and creates new memories. There are brain training programmes, such as brainteasers and puzzles that can improve memory, concentration, reflexes and the ability to multi-task.

We have the power to change our brain and our life. When we relax, our brain activity slows down (known as the *Theta State*; read Chapter 5 for more details). In this state of mind, if we have positive thoughts then we can get rid of a wrong idea, escape from a pattern of failure, poor health or a profound sense of unhappiness and fulfill our desires instead. See also Chapters 5, 10 and 21.

The Second Brain

According to Pierre Pallardy, the author of 'Gut Instinct', the second brain is situated in our intestines. It is commonly referred to as a *gut feeling* or *instinct*. An odd urge, a funny tingle, sweaty palms, a peculiar feeling in our stomach or that little voice in our head: these are our gut feelings telling us something. But what do they mean and should we take notice of them? Here's how to make the most of our inborn wisdom. Most of us have experienced knowing something before we ever come across it, even if we can't explain how. For example, we hesitate at a green light and miss getting hit by a speeding truck. If we could tap into these insights more often, it would greatly help improve the quality of our life. We can, if we learn to identify which signals to focus on.

As well, we feel intuitions in our chest or a 'burning sensation' in our gut or the intestines which house the *Enteric Nervous System*, sometimes called the 'second brain'. The second brain really is the intuitive brain, and when it speaks, we listen.

According to many researchers, the intuitive right hemisphere of the brain is almost always 'reading' our surroundings, even when our conscious left hemisphere is otherwise engaged. The body can register this information while the conscious mind remains blissfully unaware of what's going on.

Another theory suggests that we can 'feel' approaching events specifically because of our *Dopamine Neurons*. These are the neurotransmitters in the central nervous system, acting within the brain to help regulate movement and emotions. The pulsation of *dopamine*, i.e. the nerve's transmitters, helps keep track of reality, alerting us to those subtle patterns of life that we can't consciously detect.

The inter-connection of brain and heart

We also need to discuss the connections between our brain and heart. We may have heard of the *triune* (three in one) brain: reptilian (the brain stem), mammalian (the limbic, which is emotional and cognitive), and primate (the neo-cortex, which gives us our verbal and intellectual abilities). In the last 40 years or so, researchers have identified a fourth part of our brain, the prefrontal cortex. This is responsible for the blending and integration of the other parts of the brain. It is the executive centre of the brain.

However, that is not the end of the story. There is a fifth stage involving the heart, about 60-65% of which is made of neurons. These connect with the limbic system, that is to say the emotional brain, part of the right hemisphere. This hemisphere is responsible for dreaming, intuition, and creativity, the activities often attributed to the soul. See also Chapter 7.

Remember!

Both our brain and powers of intuition are amazing tools which can guide us towards our goals.

We have the ability to change our reality into a better certainty by slowing down our brain activity i.e. entering the theta state of mind.

Listen to our second brain; it must be calling for a good reason.

4
The Conscious Mind

What is the mind?

Philosophers, physicians, poets, scientists, and, of course, the rest of us, are equally perplexed by the enigma, which is the mind. Most of us, however, can sense its existence. But where is the mind? It is everywhere, so there is no need to search for our mind. It is in every cell of our body – all 50 trillion of them. In other words, our body houses over 50 trillion living organisms and is like a universe unto itself.

All minds, conscious, unconscious and the infinite are all one; we do not have separate minds but just different domains of activity within a limitless consciousness. For example, our conscious mind thinks logically. With it, we make all our day to day decisions: choosing our new house, a car or whatever else. As well, all knowledge can be obtained from the vast consciousness through numerous forms of meditation as explained in Chapters 10 and 21. However, bodily functions like breathing, digestion and blood circulation are automatically run by our unconscious mind.

The vastness of the human mind can be compared with an iceberg. The conscious mind, the little master, is the tip just above the surface. The unconscious mind, the big master, is the gigantic bulk of the iceberg hidden from sight. The sea is the supreme consciousness or the source mind. The human mind is generally considered as being divided into the conscious – when we are wide awake, deliberately making a choice or intentionally doing something – and the unconscious. The latter is when we are not truly aware of what we are doing. This is when we carry out certain actions without even really choosing to do so. For example, this is the state of mind we often experience when driving, automatically changing gears, checking the rear view mirror or using the indicator. The conscious mind is also known as the '*ego mind*' and controls our thoughts and perceptions.

The unconscious mind, the '*superego mind*', has two levels. At the *preconscious* or *subconscious* level, the mind keeps our memories and acquired knowledge, exercises the imagination, triggers off our emotions and generates our creative powers. All of these can become part of the conscious mind as we concentrate on and develop our impulses, so that they grow into concrete ideas.

At the lower level, our unconscious mind retains our fears, desires, urges, motives, and deep-rooted beliefs. This part of our unconscious mind influences our behaviour in everything that we do, for example, thinking, reading, imagining, etc. Any type of behaviour that is observable, that we are aware of, is defined as being *overt* or *conscious*, for example, talking, eating, etc. On the other hand, any type of behaviour that is internal and therefore not perceptible, which we do not notice, is classed as *covert* or *unconscious*. For example, without realising it, if we have been standing for a while we shift our balance from one side to the other, so as to give a rest, relatively speaking, to one of our legs.

Although we are individual in form, we are a part of a much larger whole. The cells within our body are the same. They are individual, microscopic forms of life that exist independently of one another, but collectively exist as a whole, and in turn make up our body. We know this from the latest research into micro-cellular structure. For example, according to Dr. Bruce Lipton PHD, a cellular biologist at Stanford University School of Medicine, the cells in our body are individual sentient beings that have the ability and the capacity to hold memories just as we do on a larger scale.

In other words, cells have the capacity to store memories within themselves. This is called cellular level memory. Just as we hold memories of past events, conditions and circumstances and this is part of our unconscious mind, so do the cells of our body. Memories of past beliefs, positive or negative, affect our health and prosperity. A limiting belief, for instance, 'I am not worthy of receiving all the good things that have been made available to me,' will affect our life chances adversely. All pessimistic thoughts and attitudes weaken our immune system, causing ill-health as well as low self-esteem.

There are two fundamental functions of our mind. One is to control our conscious or daily activities, which we are fully aware of, such as taking a shower or washing dishes. Thus the concept of the *'conscious mind'* was created.

The other function relates to all the activities controlled on a default or automated basis by our non-conscious or unconscious mind. We act like a robot that is following a set programme. When we are not paying attention to an action, then it is performed through our unconscious default system or memory. This happens, for example, when riding a bike or the automatic responses of the human body, such as breathing more quickly during exercise. It is not a thought-out or creative process. We have to consciously desire what we want, because otherwise we will encounter the likes of fear, greed and danger. These will be drawn to us on a default basis from our overpowering unconscious mind.

So we have two minds! Have we ever tried to change our mind, only to find out that our mind has a mind of its own? For example, the last time we decided to get into shape or we made a New Year's resolution to quit smoking but could not.

The conscious mind operates on will; it sets goals, judges results and likes to try new things. It is a 'feeling mind'. Our good feelings are a kind of positive energy and our bad feelings emit negative energy. To feel good, we have to change the negative energy into positive. (Chapter 16 explains how to feel good and be happy.)

Our conscious mind has a short term memory with a limited processing capacity. Through the power of our conscious mind we focus, choose to be more optimistic and feel more positive. We are co-creators with the supreme creator, creating reality through thoughts held in our conscious mind. What a mind can conceive and **believe as true**, a mind can receive. If we don't believe we can achieve something, our negative thoughts will make sure we don't achieve it. The power of our own mind is a gift from the Creator – so we must take possession of our mind.

Everything comes to us through the most elemental law of physics – as we sow, so shall we reap, water always flows downstream, like attracts like! As they say, birds of a feather flock together. Feelings of anxiety and hatred attract experiences that make us feel depressed. Conversely, positive emotions such as a longing for peace, love, kindness and gratitude make us feel contented.

Remember, like attracts like. This is an absolute law and has nothing to do with our personality, religious beliefs, being a 'good' or a 'bad' person or anything else. No one lives beyond this law. It is one of the unquestionable laws of the universe. It reinforces that which we shall become, according to our predominant thoughts; seek and we shall find, knock and a door shall open. 'Ask, and it is given' – there is no more powerful statement. This is the most fundamental reason why things happen the way they do. Asking with real desire summons the creative force!

We attract whatever we focus on, whether it is desirable or not. What we focus on is what we attract. Focus on success and we will be successful. Focusing on what might go wrong, can only result in failure. If we think about being broke, poor, lonely and believe our thoughts, guess what? That is exactly what we'll be. This law applies to our life and every other person's life on the planet. Like all laws, it is impersonal and impartial. This means it works whether we want it to or not. For more on this concept, read Chapter 11.

The scientific view of the mind

Physical science has divided matter into molecules, molecules into atoms, atoms into energy. Neuroscientist, Jill Bolte Taylor, of Harvard University, has stated that we are all connected in this universe of energy. This point is further explained by Sir Ambrose Fleming, in an address before the Royal Institution, declaring this energy as the spirit of the mind. He says: 'In its ultimate essence, energy may be incomprehensible by us except as an exhibition of the direct operation of that which we call mind or will.' The mind is composed of the energy that interpenetrates the brain and body. As well, as Jeffrey Eugenides, novelist and short story writer, puts it, 'Biology gives you a brain. Life turns it into a mind.'

Dr. Bob Rhondell Gibson, author of *Notes on Personal Integration and Health*, states that there are four levels of consciousness: waking, dreaming, sleeping and the quantum or universal consciousness. The mind functions at an unseen, sub-atomic state. After all, we cannot see our thoughts, each one being a unique seed which can grow and create. Just like a seed has the potential to become a tree, the zygote, a tiny speck of protein and what we are at the moment of our conception, knows all about every other living thing in the universe!

The universe is made up of energy which is constantly flowing. The nature of life itself is continual change. The purest form of energy, according to scientists who study quantum physics, is what they refer to as wave forms of probability that exist within an infinite field of probabilities. Einstein's theorems proved that all things – e.g. sound, thoughts, emotions and any physical entity – exist only as a result of this pure energy.

We need to keep our conscious mind busy by expecting the best. This means we must make sure our thoughts concentrate on what we want to see happen in our life. The mind is a creature of habit. Our mind will help us find success, happiness, health and prosperity, when those desires are what we habitually think about.

Remember!

Our mind is the faculty of thought and consciousness. It enables us to be aware of the world.

Our thoughts are creative.

Always expect the best for ourselves in our daily thinking.

What we focus on is what we will become.

5

The Unconscious Mind

The term *the unconscious mind* was first coined by the 18th century German-born romantic philosopher Sir Christopher Riegel, and later popularised by the poet and essayist Samuel Taylor Coleridge.

The unconscious mind (or simply the unconscious) consists of mental processes which occur automatically. Experimental evidence suggests that the unconscious mind gives rise to a collection of mental activities that emerge, but which the person is not aware of at the time. For example, unconscious thoughts can lead to seemingly inexplicable phobias. Our life is a reflection of the unconscious or hidden beliefs we have. The mind is a reservoir of all possibilities and the most powerful part of it, the unconscious mind, rests untouched below the surface like an iceberg. In reality, it is the deepest and greatest part of the mind and considerably influences decision-making, the different ways in which we conduct ourselves and, indeed, how we live our lives. It is the fortress of memories, feelings and thoughts, of everything we have ever been aware of. Therefore, it is knowledgeable and powerful in a different way from the conscious mind. For example, sometimes, we forget someone's name. Suddenly, a day or two later, without having tried to do so, we remember the name.

I believe the greatest breakthrough of the 19th century was not in the realm of the physical sciences, but rather the discovery of the power of the unconscious mind, when it is touched by faith. Here, faith means complete trust or confidence – or seeing with our heart what our eyes can't see. Anyone can tap into this eternal reservoir of power. This can then enable any of us to overcome any problems that may arise. Each individual world which we inhabit can be shaped by our thoughts and beliefs. (For more on the role of belief in our life, read Chapter 9.) All weaknesses can be overcome (for example, recovering from illness, financial independence, the need for spiritual awakening,) beyond our wildest dreams.

Our unconscious mind controls the body's motor functions, as well as the heart rate and digestion etc. It stores past experiences, different modes of behaviour, attitudes and values and is permanent. It works mostly through images, sounds, and smells. However, it does not work logically. Therefore, it cannot understand words like 'don't' or 'not'. For example, if you give someone the simple instruction: *Don't think about a red car!* What happens? The person thinks about **a red car**! The unconscious mind is, in a sense, our closest companion, but it has no filtering system. We only have to understand that the unconscious mind simply does what it does. So, we have to guide our own unconscious mind in a clear and precise manner.

The unconscious mind works best when we are apparently not alert or active; for instance, when we are sleeping. Similarly, it also functions well when we are relaxed. Often, we experience that eureka moment in the bath or while staring into space. At times, such as these, we suddenly experience a moment of enlightenment. There will definitely be numerous examples when, without focusing on anything in particular, we are, in an instant, inspired. A brilliant idea, as if from nowhere, enters our mind. Think of Isaac Newton, sitting underneath a tree. An apple falls on his head – the discovery of gravity!

The unconscious mind only understands anything when it is in the present tense. Expressing a goal in the present tense – *as if it has already been achieved* – can take a bit of getting used to. We may feel like we're lying to ourselves, but it's a necessary step because of the way the unconscious handles instructions. In other words, it's like 'fake it until we make it'. Think, talk and act as if our goal were already a reality. For example, say to ourselves: 'I am getting better every day,' or, 'I love to succeed at whatever I choose.'

As well, the unconscious mind possesses a vast store of memories and can deal with thousands of events, on average 4 billion bits of information per second. It's easier to change habitual thoughts and behaviour if we access the unconscious mind, because it is the repository of attitudes, values and beliefs. It has a memory of every event we have ever experienced. Scientific research has demonstrated that when we remember an event, that particular memory is updated with our life experiences. Memories are the result of information that we have taken in over a lifetime of experiences, although the memories which influence us the most were formed before we were six years old.

When we are thinking about a future outcome, it is as if we are creating **a memory of an event in advance of it happening**. We are biologically creating a synaptic neural pathway (simply put, connecting one part of the nervous system with another,) to fire this future event before it occurs. Charles Perrow, a renowned sociologist states, 'You are creating a world that is congruent with your interpretation, even though it may be wrong.' In other words, we are creating our own reality or realm in agreement with our thoughts, which can result in a positive (*right*) or a negative (*wrong*) outcome.

Our unconscious mind is also the source of our emotions, which result from our day to day experiences. Whatever happens to us controls the way we behave. All this, in turn, colours the way we see ourselves and others. If we want to change for the better we have to change or manage our behaviour. The great German poet and scholar, Johann Wolfgang von Goethe, got it right some two hundred years ago, when he wrote, *'Behaviour is the mirror, in which everyone shows their image.'* Of course, we reveal ourselves, perhaps far more than we realise, through our behaviour. Our habits are a kind of automatic behaviour which we acquire and practise in steps. The unconscious mind stores all our different kinds of behaviour as programmes and runs them automatically.

It's easier to change any kind of behaviour if we access the unconscious mind because this is where such attitudes, values and beliefs are held. This is why we can change any behaviour through reflection, relaxation and meditation. Once we feel a change in our behaviour, **then in turn this changes the behaviour of others towards us.**

It is vital to tempt or coax our unconscious mind with our desires, and before we realise, it will be our best assistant. When we have our unconscious mind on our side, there is no painful struggle; it's all fun and joy. Always think, for example, 'wouldn't it be cool if I had funds to buy my dream red 7 series BMW?' Or 'Wouldn't it be great if I had bought that house I viewed in France?' For more exciting guidance in this regard, read Chapter 10 and Chapter 11.

By relaxing, we can fulfil our desires. When it comes to programming our unconscious mind, the best way is to be patient. Can we see the subtle difference in this way of thinking? We are not forcing our unconscious mind, but tempting it. The way forward is to be relaxed, calm and trusting. The answer will come to us. There's no point in trying to rush things. Sooner or later, we will be guided to the right answer. For example, if we misplace our keys, we start to search for them frantically. Something, our intuition, tells us go to bedroom and there we find them.

This is a true story. On Saturday 4th July 2015, at approximately 8:30 a.m., my son, Zain, told me, 'I can't find my bus pass. Can you please drop me in town?'

I replied, 'Sorry, I am not ready. Keep looking for it.' With exasperation, I added, 'Didn't you use it last night?'

He had another go, without success. He came back to me, and said he still couldn't find the bus pass.

'Okay. Call for your bus card. Say, where are you, my bus card?'

As soon as I finished my sentence, he shouted, 'Oh, I've found it!'

The card was lying on the floor near his right foot.

Thinking in this way means we don't become anxious about getting whatever we desire. This adds to our already rich and happy life. That's how self-made people think, i.e. they relax and quietly trust the infinite consciousness. If we keep thinking this way, soon all our actions will be joyful and our desires will become reality. We can see an example of this in the hugely successful career of Bill Gates, who has often experienced his greatest moments of insight and inspiration away from the workplace. However, these benefits only accrue when we use our free time to let our imagination soar.

The greatest power of all is our unconscious mind. We don't need to acquire this power – we already possess it. It's believed 95% of our decisions are made in our unconscious mind and then sent to our conscious mind. It receives the thought 1/3 of a second after our unconscious mind has already made the decision.

The unconscious mind is changeable; it is only a storehouse. Metaphorically, we can go in there. As Dr Bruce Harold Lipton puts it, 'You have a choice to change.' He is an American developmental biologist best known for promoting the idea that genes and DNA do not control our biology; that instead DNA is controlled by signals from outside the cell, including the energetic messages emanating from our positive and negative thoughts.

So, first of all, it is necessary to identify and question the beliefs we want to change. The moment we begin to question our beliefs and the experiences we assign to them, we no longer feel absolutely certain about them. This opens the door to replacing our old, disempowering beliefs with new ones that will support us in the direction we want to go.

We have to say to ourselves repeatedly, '**I can always find the best way forward, if I really want to.' This is also an example of auto-suggestion.** By repeating to ourselves the suggestion we wish to accept, we impress the unconscious mind, making it believe in our intentions and goals. Dear reader, for this very reason, you will notice that there is deliberately some repetition of the different concepts presented in this book. Repetition is the mother of skill; it reinforces concepts over and over again.

A real life example of autosuggestion is as follows. My friend's son was a pupil at a rather expensive private school. He was not happy there. Indeed, he would much rather have been studying in an ordinary state school. For perfectly obvious reasons, this annoyed the private school's Head Teacher. Eventually, the young man changed schools, but not before the Head Teacher told him, 'I bet you'll achieve nothing in that school.'

A little while later I met my friend's son. I asked him how things were at school.

He told me that he was in the ninth year and much preferred where he was to his old school. He then added, 'The previous head was really nasty to me.' He then explained to me what this man had said and how it still really upset him.

I gave him the following piece of advice: 'Write down that insult on some paper. Then straightaway cross it out completely. Next, write something positive to replace the abusive remark, such as, *I can pass easily and I will.*'

He did as he was told. This simple act changed his attitude towards success and failure and today he is studying at a top university. As well, he still keeps the same piece of paper in his wallet!

By converting those negative beliefs and emotions which make us fail in real life into positive ones, we can succeed. For example, when we don't believe we look sick, we are not affected by what others think.

Being aware that their mental image of us is not the same as ours, gives us immunity to their opinion. By understanding this, it is obvious that we cannot be hurt emotionally by what others think and say about us.

Once we understand this and learn to use the power within ourselves, we can create wonderful changes and achieve many goals. Now, this idea may sound scary, that every negative unconscious thought is drawn into our life. But we shouldn't worry, because the reverse also happens. Every joyful thought we have, can also become a part of our life.

'Cultivate the habit of making aware choice. Your choice makes your destiny. Do not be carried away by the unconscious choices.'
– Amit Ray – author and spiritual master.

How can we access this power of our unconscious? Is there a **key**? Yes – the theta level of our mind. This can be reached through meditation. Scientists have done a lot of research about the functions of the brain. The electrical impulses emitted continuously by the brain keep changing their frequency depending on the activity involved. This is measured by equipment called EEG in cycles per second.

Theta brain waves (4–8Hz) are present during deep meditation, light sleep and when we dream. The theta level is within the unconscious mind and is also known as the twilight state. This is the point where the verbal/thinking mind transitions to the meditative/visual mind. The theta state is associated with visualisation. Having a vivid imagination, or experiencing some form of remarkable inspiration, profound creativity, exceptional insight, as well as the mind's most deep-seated beliefs are all part of the theta state. A sense of deep spiritual connection and oneness with the universe can be experienced at this level. In addition, theta waves improve our memory and enable us to gain far more inspiration and insight. In the theta state, we can be in a waking dream, when receptivity to new ideas is heightened and we are able to access knowledge and information that normally lies beyond our conscious awareness.

In contrast with the theta brainwave, the alpha brainwave is part of the conscious mind. Although it is capable of bridging the gap between conscious thoughts and the unconscious, it is only the theta brainwave which allows us to really connect with our unconscious mind. Only then does the unconscious mind become activated. This level can be reached with simple meditation and relaxation techniques. By progressively relaxing first the body and then the mind, the theta brainwaves begin to function. One simple method is to focus on the breathing. The breath and mind work in tandem. Therefore, as our breathing slows down, our brain waves begin to lengthen.

First of all, we sit comfortably with our shoulders relaxed and with a straight spine. We then place our hands on our lap and close eyes and forget about all our worries, by concentrating on positive thoughts. We should notice how our breath flows in and out. We mustn't try to change this in any way, but we need to take note of how it happens. If our mind begins to wander, we have to start thinking about our breathing again. We will soon realise that each breath is getting longer and beginning to fill our body. Our mind becomes completely calm. We are now in the theta state of mind. As the mind relaxes, it is elevated and can accept change far more readily, so that we will find the answers we need. (For more detail, read Chapters 10 and 21.)

Remember!

The unconscious mind is a massive storehouse of information and controls including our beliefs that run our life on autopilot.

It is always alert and awake. It is listening even when we are asleep.

It takes in everything literally. So, we need to be careful about what we say. If we say, 'I feel bad,' it may be true, but don't say it. Instead, we have to say something more positive, such as, 'I'll soon feel better.'

Our unconscious only knows the here and now. When we set up our goal, phrase it in the present tense, as if it is being already achieved.

Regardless of our past, if we truly believe we can achieve something – we're most of the way there already.

Meditation is an incredibly useful tool to use, when we want to succeed in life.

6

Consciousness

What is consciousness? That which can't be imagined, but without which there can't be imagination; that which cannot be thought of but without which there is no thinking, that which cannot be perceived or identified, but without which there is nothing.

The infinite consciousness is alive and we are part of it. When we look at ourselves in the mirror, what do we see? Is it the real me or the person I have been conditioned into believing is the real me? For all of us, our real self is part of the infinite consciousness, which allows us to create or to be whatever we want. The other self is a product of other people's definitions and pre-conceived notions. This is the false self, held back, incapable of fulfilling our vast potential.

All we can know of the world in an absolute sense comes from our own sensory perceptions and the mental constructions we build around them. Behind these lies the vast consciousness. Indeed, quantum physicists have shown that this immeasurable consciousness is the basic substance of the entire universe.

The Divine or Nature's plan is very simple. It assumes two things from us: it wants us to flourish and be happy. We are a part of Nature's plentiful energies.

'I am large, I contain multitudes.' – Walt Whitman, American Poet.

Metaphorically speaking, in the same way, each ray of light is connected to the sun and every drop of water to the oceans. We are born worthy of all things, free of judgements; being enriched in every sense is our natural state. Our state of mind is our state of being, our infinite capacity to be. This is a temporary state of thought, in which one has to be, rather than artificially creating it. For example, we can be wealthy or happy. Our state of being is found in the way we think. How we achieve this is up to us. Only then can we follow our desires.

Nature works with both easy and endless precision. We don't have to understand how our happiness or wealth is created. **We must always, simply think, speak and act according to our vision. Then everything will come true.** It's wrong to resist whatever happens along the way. **This is nature's way of bringing to us what we visualise. We need to respond with feelings of excitement and joy.** We have to keep our dreams big.

The limitless consciousness is like a search engine, finding what we want. It passes down to the unconscious mind all this information. In turn, the unconscious mind is always listening, feeling and reacting to every one of these stimuli.

In this realm of infinite possibilities, everything already exists. It is listening to everything we ask or pray for and everything we think of or choose. It can only give us what we give it to work with. So when we desire anything, do so in absolute detail. It will figure out the HOW because the consciousness already holds all the answers. We hand over the rest to our internal Sat-Nav system i.e. the inexhaustible consciousness; it is a supreme guidance system and, therefore, infallible. Read also Chapter 17.

Until recently, the predominant view of scientists has been materialist. Space, time, and matter constitute reality and consciousness somehow arises from this. The truth now appears to be the opposite. Even in the reality we have experienced so far, consciousness is of primary importance.

However, time, space, and matter are secondary; they are aspects of an image of reality forming in the mind. They exist within our consciousness; not the other way around. If we consider the reality we experience, then we have to accept that in the final analysis, the new age physicists and writers, like Murray Gell-Mann and Arthur Koestler, are correct: consciousness is the essence of everything in the known universe. Through our consciousness we experience everything.

'The key to growth is the introduction of higher dimensions of consciousness into our awareness.' – Lao Tzu, philosopher and poet of Ancient China.

For example, finding our purpose and then sharing it with the rest of the world, or spending time with friends who share our beliefs and our values, or taking conscious control of all our decisions, or being compassionate and forgiving towards ourselves, or becoming more aware of our breathing through exercises like meditation, or walking, connecting and appreciating nature in the forest etc. will continue to raise our level of consciousness.

How is it that consciousness, which doesn't physically exist, can take on the material forms of experience? How do all the physical aspects of the material world emerge in our consciousness?

The answer is something we all share. This is our consciousness. This is an undeniable truth. Our consciousness is always present in every experience we have, the essence of everything we know. Therefore, it creates the world as we understand it.

We traditionally associate truth, absoluteness, eternity and of course creation with the Creator. From this perspective, the statement 'I am also a creator or co-creator' is not so puzzling or deluded after all.

What is consciousness? It is the ultimate source of our being.

Here is an example. Just visualise that we are riding a horse. The horse symbolises our creator, the higher self, our source, or whatever word we have for it. As we direct our life, we pull the reins to the left and the horse goes left. If we pull the reins to the right, it goes right. This is how free will works. We decide something and then it happens. It all works fine as long as the *horse* goes in the direction we want it to. However, the problem starts when the horse disobeys us and careers off in another direction.

Here we find ourselves in the realm of hypothesis and speculation: Maybe we did something wrong; maybe the Creator (the horse) doesn't want us to take this path; maybe we are just not strong-willed enough. However, we will never find a satisfactory explanation.

What happens on a spiritual level of understanding is as follows:

As we and our higher self (the horse) are one, the signal (our intuition) originally comes from our higher self and in agreement with that we pull the horse left or right. Whenever we hear the signal and we follow it, we are absolutely in agreement with our higher self, our source, our infinite power.

Is this still free will? We may ask. Yes, it is, as it is still we who are giving ourselves the signal. This is a profound and powerful concept when we truly understand it. All that it takes to operate our life on this level is to explore our consciousness and understand that it is infinite and the ultimate source of our being. It is a wonderful experience to have this power at our command.

Remember!

The infinite consciousness is always listening, feeling and reacting and we are part of it. We must look within ourselves for the answers to our heart's desire.

Have we ever tried asking ourselves prior to sleep, 'I want to wake up at 5 a.m.'? It's the inexhaustible consciousness that wakes us up at the right time.

There are no limits to our potential.

When we visualise and live according to our aspirations, they will come about. It is nature's way of making real what we envisage.

The boundless consciousness is like a search engine; it locates what we desire and passes it on to us.

7

The Heart

'The heart is a strange beast and not ruled by logic.'
– Maria V. Snyder, award winning fantasy author.

'Follow your heart, but be quiet for a while first. Ask questions, and then feel the answer. Learn to trust your heart.'
– James Earl Jones, actor.

We used to believe that the mind or consciousness resided in the heart. Words like sweetheart, hard-hearted, kind-hearted, you are my heart, etc. originated from this erroneous belief. Physicians, led by the Canadian brain surgeon, Wilder Graves Penfield, 1891–1976, tried to locate the conscious mind in the brain. They did succeed in identifying how certain parts of the brain control particular bodily functions.

When we have a feeling in our heart, we are creating electrical and magnetic signals inside of our body that extend into the world around us. The heart cells are unique in that they produce strong electromagnetic signals extending as far as twelve to fifteen feet from the body in the shape of a torus (a ring-shaped object, like a doughnut).

These toroidal fields are very important. There are two fields within the centre of our heart. Although shaped like a doughnut, there is no empty central 'hole'. These fields are intimately connected to all our experiences at the deepest level of understanding. 'This torus function is apparently holographic, meaning that any point within the torus contains the information of the whole field.' – Itzhak Bentov, scientist and inventor.

Indeed, the torus is our connection to the eternal realm. In fact, the earth's magnetic field, the solar system, perhaps, the universe itself, are formed in the shape of a torus.

Some scientists, for example Rita Gott Marr, life coach and

metaphysical physician, conjecture that all energy systems from the atomic to the universal level are toroid in form. Therefore, it is possible there is one torus encompassing an infinite number of interacting, holographic tori within its spectrum, from the universal to the individual mind and heart.

A feeling (positive or negative) by definition is the union of thought and emotion. Our heart is constantly sending information to our body. Every beat carries critical messages that affect our emotional and physical health. A negative feeling harms our physical health. We all know that feelings like anger, jealousy and hatred can take their toll on our mind and spirit. Negative emotions can also suppress the immune system, increase stress levels, cause the heart to beat faster, blood pressure to rise, and even affect the heart's electrical stability, all of which can lead to heart disease and strokes.

Conversely, scientists have shown that love, gratitude or appreciation boosts our immune system. Dr Barbara Fredrickson, professor of psychology at the University of North Carolina, has spent years researching the physical and emotional benefits of feeling positive. Not only do positive attitudes benefit health and wellbeing, but also we can strengthen them with practice. These positive emotions literally reverse the physical effects of negativity and build up our psychological resources, which in turn help us succeed.

These findings remind me of when my friend, a successful estate agent, was ill.

One day, he explained to me that he was going to have a heart bypass operation. 'I'm so worried,' he said, 'not only about my business, but, far more importantly, about my children.'

I suggested to him that whenever a thought to do with any 'bypass operation' came into his head, he had to cancel it out by saying quietly to himself, 'I will be okay.' He followed my suggestion and soon was no longer afraid of the operation or any of its possible consequences.

Although he had to undergo a second operation, he has had a long successful career, his children are grown up and successful in their own right and he remains healthy and happy.

When we experience love, compassion, understanding or forgiveness, our heart is sending a powerful electromagnetic signal. Our heartbeat is detectable in the brain waves of the other person! The same beneficial effect occurs in our body when love and appreciation are transmitted toward us from someone else. The best and most beautiful things in the world cannot be seen or even touched – they must come from the heart and enter another person's mind.

When we project our emotions, either positive or negative, into our thoughts, we make those thoughts become reality. Those two energies (thoughts and emotions) meet in the one centre that is our heart. They create our feelings.

Interestingly, our heart creates the strongest electro-magnetic fields in our body. They are much stronger than those in our brain. These magnetic fields change according to our feelings. In this way, we alter our physical reality.

The more we understand the human heart, the more we influence reality. This, however, is not achieved through the process of thinking. Thoughts are important but these feelings are in the centre of our heart.

When many people gather together united by one common feeling, they can change the world.

We already know our imagination is of great importance. However, what we imagine, is often fleeting. Our heart-based feelings are far more powerful.

'The brain gives the heart its sight. The heart gives the brain its vision.' – Rob Kall, counselling psychologist.

Our prayers, requests, beliefs and even self-expression, when from the heart, all directly affect our body and the world around us.

Many of us know laughter is the language of the heart. The more we laugh, the more our heart opens up. Thus, we gain more quickly our heart's desire. It's possible to overcome all our problems and create our ideal life through our heart.

The heart is the doorway to true power, the key to creation. In fact, if we're not working with or aware of this energetic field, we're really missing out because this power is absolutely astonishing.

'A decision is made with the brain. A commitment is made with the heart. Therefore, a commitment is much deeper and more binding than a decision.' – Nido Qubein, businessman and motivational speaker.

So what we choose to experience, we must first feel in our heart, as if it is already happening. Our inner world (i.e. our thoughts, feelings, emotions and beliefs) can affect our lives. Our inner experiences can influence the world beyond, through the consciousness or the universal, intelligent mind.

We can change our self-esteem and our body will mirror that change. It will happen at its own tempo. Remember, none of us can change anything for the better overnight. We have to avoid unrealistic expectations and instead take small steps forward, while at the same time still focusing on our dreams. Whatever or whoever created us made us a part of the same energy that created the entire universe. Therefore, we are all capable of using that profound life force to change our lives, according to our own will.

If we want to change something then:

1. Pose questions beginning with words like, '*Why can't, why not, what if, what else is available* or *what would be best for me?*' Read also Chapter 17.

2. We have to change the internal programming that exists deep within our unconscious mind. To do this we must get rid of any habitual, negative self-talk. Again, see Chapter 17.

'Remember that wherever your heart is, there you will find your treasure.' – Paulo Coelho, lyricist and novelist.

Remember!

The heart is our most unexploited source. Utilise its limitless power and create the things that we wish for in our life.

Avoid negative feelings like anger and jealousy that create stress. Enjoy the feelings of gratitude and love and live a happy life.

The heart generates electro-magnetic energy. By exploiting this energy, we can create a glittering future.

Don't let the brain rule the heart. Make use of our intuition. It comes from the heart.

PART THREE

Knowledge is Power

8. Thoughts Become Reality

9. Belief

10. Imagination

11. The Need to Focus

12. Intentions

13. Gratitude

14. Forgiveness: Letting go of our Anger

15. Allowing Life to Flow Effortlessly

16. Reasons to Feel Contented

8
Thoughts Become Reality

What we accept as the truth is the person we are. In other words, we always become what we believe. Imagine our unconscious is 'the soil' of our 'mental garden', in which the seeds of thought are planted. Surrender to that the all-knowing presence of the Creator to bring to fruition, in the perfect way and at the right time, what we desire. The Creator knows exactly what to do, what adjustments must be made, what elements must be harvested and just when to bring everything together. Remember, positive thoughts make us an optimist and negative ones a pessimist.

'The power of positive thinking is directly connected with the ability to eliminate negative thoughts. Doubts, fears, focusing on what could go wrong and the like, are clear signs of negative thinking. Such thoughts can eventually destroy our life. We could think of them of being choking weeds – and 'don't water your weeds', as Harvey MacKay, businessman and author, puts it.

We mustn't worry! Instead we have to focus on what we want, rather than what we **don't** want. This is because the *law of manifestation* works on the principle of '*like attracts like*'. Our thoughts attract our physical experiences, because the mental plane is really just a higher degree of the physical plane.

Imagine how much we've changed in the last ten years. After all, nothing in creation can ever stay the same. At the same time, this tells us that we can also change our own self-image and that's exactly what we need to do.

In other words, we have to think more highly of ourselves and trust ourselves more. Just as we learn new things, the older we become, we can also gain in self-confidence at the same time. There is no point in mulling over the past or in fearing the future; we can only live in the present. By focusing on the here and now, we improve the quality of our life.

'Do not wait for life. Do not long for it. Be aware, always and at every moment that the miracle is in the here and now.' – Marcel Proust, novelist, critic, and essayist.

Therefore, success is a state of mind. By creating positive thinking patterns, we will be far more successful. Our unconscious mind brings us **the people, situations and circumstances** to help us succeed. We could start by writing a list of possible ideas we could pursue. We should never be afraid of experimenting and then evaluating the results. We simply need to see which ones work and discard those which don't. The successful ones could easily lead to new habits and even beliefs. These, in turn, are impressed on the unconscious mind and help us succeed. This is the power of positive thinking.

External circumstances are not really important. All the events in our life, whatever they might be, mirror our thoughts. Life is exactly how we picture it to be. That's why, if we want to change our life, we must first of all start by changing our thoughts. Thoughts and intentions – after all, intentions are merely thoughts – are physical 'some-things' with the astonishing power to change our world. Every thought we have, generates its own energy. Thought itself is a form of energy. To create it, a thought is given a symbolic or abstract form, i.e. a mental picture. That's why we must be positive! In this way, we can believe anything is possible.

Self-evidently, thoughts can be very powerful. Without hopefully belabouring the obvious, they are the source of all our creativity. However, what makes our thoughts truly powerful is emotion. As soon as thoughts become emotions, they also become reality, whether for good or ill. Thoughts inspired by love will produce miracles in our life. Thoughts stimulated by fear will have devastating consequences.

Love is the most powerful emotion we can experience. Yet it is so much more; it is a way of being. It connects us to a plane beyond any physical experience. Anything we desire, we desire because we would 'love' to have it. When a thought is filled with love, it will bring forth that which we desire in the most amazing way.

Conversely, when our thoughts are corrupted by fear, what we fear will come to pass. Because of an incident from my teens, I know this to be true. My cousin wanted to learn how to ride a bike. I took him to our school playground. It was safe there. With the help of two of my friends we put my cousin on the bike and gently pushed him along.

Suddenly he shouted, 'Oh, there is puddle over there and I am going to fall in it!'

I replied, 'Well! It's too far away. Ignore it.'

He kept calling for help, as he was completely obsessed with the puddle. That's why he ended up falling in to it…

On a more serious note, if we fear being poor, we will be poor, until we change how we think.

Feeling pleased at the potential benefits of the thing we want are thoughts made into emotions. Such thoughts become dominant and increase our desire for what we want. Thus, we behave and act in a manner which leads us to our goal. As well, these thoughts determine our level of success, as they easily enter into our unconscious mind.

The unconscious mind is more susceptible to the influence of these emotional thoughts. In fact, we all know that only thoughts suffused with emotion have any real influence upon the unconscious mind. It is essential, therefore, that we understand the method of approach to this 'inner audience'. We must speak its language, or it will not heed our call. It understands best the language of emotion. Only feed the unconscious with positive emotions, such as, faith, hope and love. Never forget to avoid the negative emotions of fear, greed or jealousy.

'Hope is the fuel of progress and fear is the prison in which you put yourself.' – Tony Benn, politician.

Let's train ourselves to have positive emotions! For example, if we want to feel more confident – stand tall, breathe deeply, speak more clearly. Eventually, positive feelings will dominate our mind and all negative thoughts will be banished.

On the other hand, if we're not happy with our life and things aren't going the way we want, then simply track our thoughts, so as to understand how our own mind-set might be defeating us in our endeavours, even before we try to succeed. That's why, if we regularly think that it's difficult to find a job, we'll probably have a hard time finding a job. In other words, every one of our thoughts and words create our future.

'The best way to predict your future is to create.' – Abraham Lincoln, Sixteenth President of the United States of America.

Our thoughts transcend the universe, are accepted by our unconscious mind and return to us as experiences. That's why we must be aware of what we're thinking. Much of our belief system resides in our unconscious mind. We are not aware of it; these are the things bred into us as a child. Therefore, we all ought to take a little time to figure out what they are. Then we should ask ourselves seriously, are these unspoken and unchallenged assumptions the basis for the way we wish to lead our life? In other words, we must reiterate that we can change our life when we confront our conscious mind.

Our mind is a tool, but it can be much more than that. We may think that our mind controls everything, but it's only that we have been trained to think this way. The way we use our mind now is merely as a slave to habit. We can retrain our mind. Indeed, we can use our mind in any way we want, making ourselves aware of what we are thinking. We do this simply by asking ourselves often, 'What am I thinking? Would I like this thought to control my life? Does this thought represent the experience I really want?' Admittedly, it does take a while to attain this state of conscious creativity, but it's certainly worth the effort.

We can control our thoughts if we are prepared to change our life. In this way, we can find prosperity.

Feeling good about ourselves really is the key to having a great life. When we do so, we are in tune with who we really are. Doing so means everyone else around us feels good at the same time. We spread nothing but joy.

Any success doesn't just come because we keep thinking about our goals in life. Our achievements are as a result of the emotions which underpin our thoughts. Only by combining thoughts and emotions – that is to say, our desires – is it possible to influence the unconscious mind. In this way, the emotions we feel energise our intentions. At the same time, we must value what we want. Thus, these thoughts, animated by our feelings, will pulsate with one another in harmony and together these two emotions create the power needed for us to realise our aims in life.

Everything we know of is made of this same vibrating energy – even our thoughts. Whatever vibrates at the same frequency as something else, these two things are drawn to one another. This is because the universe is interconnected by a vast energy field. This means that each one of us is connected to everyone and everything else. That's one fundamental reason why we all need to pay close attention to our thoughts, intentions and actions.

Choosing, from this immense chain of thoughts, a particular one is an act requiring a great deal of attention. Our thoughts are, of course, of immense importance because they give us images of infinite possibilities. In this realm of unending potential, everything already exists. This was already understood in the distant past. Ancient traditions invite us to grasp these possibilities with the power of our minds. As Socrates, ancient Greek philosopher, states, 'The un-contemplated life is not worth living.'

Furthermore, the most powerful forces of nature – gravity, magnetism, electricity – are invisible. In the same way, the greatest strength at the disposal of any man is invisible, as this stems from his spiritual power. The only way this spiritual force can manifest itself is through the process of thinking. That is why **what we think about envelopes our life.** Whether we see this from a scientific, spiritual, or emotional perspective, this still remains a universal truth.

That is why when we think *no* to *drugs, smoking, war, violence*, etc., these types of words are far more emotive than the simple word *no*. Emotive words always trigger off emotions in the listener or reader. Therefore, we still envisage every one of these negative concepts and allow them into our life.

Remember, *like* attracts *like*. This fundamental law of life is the cause of all past, present and future events in the lives of everyone in the world. We can find our way through the labyrinth of life, as life itself is always speaking to us. We simply need to be aware of its subtle whispers. Our intuition, the still quiet voice, our sixth sense, if we prefer, tells us the truth. We can then discover the truth in quiet contemplation, through dreams, or by being creative.

Often our intuition speaks to us in a quiet moment, unexpectedly providing us with a startling insight. For example, James Watson and his partner, Frances Crick, were researching the chemical foundations of life itself, what came to be the discovery of DNA. Watson literally dreamt of two intertwined snakes. By so doing, he interpreted correctly DNA's double helix structure.

Another example of intuition is a sense which could be termed *intuitive hearing*. Imagine we are driving along a city street and an inner voice yells, 'Stop!' We immediately brake. Within a split-second, a small child runs out in front of our car. There surely would have been a terrible accident but for this *clairaudient* experience. By the by, *clairaudient* means we 'hear' something in an abstract sense, without using our ears.

We could also, as one of our intuitive powers, being *clairsentient*. Sometimes this is simply called a *gut-feeling*. For example, when house hunting, after many hours, days, weeks… of fruitless searching, we realise in an instant we have just arrived outside our future home.

When the left hemisphere of the brain, where our powers of logic reside, is active, it tends to overwhelm our powers of intuition. To make that inner intuitive voice audible, we need to switch off from the hectic, everyday world. We can do this through day-dreaming, meditation, prayer, simply by communing with nature, or by choosing to be somewhere, where we can listen to the silence around us.

One typical example of this is of a long-time executive of a tobacco company, who, eventually, felt morally obliged to accept that the product she helped sell – kills. Preferring to remain anonymous, nevertheless, she did make public her deep sense of disquiet. She asked herself, 'How can my company publicly acknowledge the problems tobacco can create?' She kept asking this same question over and over again. One day, when she was walking in some woods, her mind focussed on nothing in particular, she suddenly, seemingly from nowhere, found the answer which had eluded her for so long. Her company would join the Corporate Social Responsibility Movement and educate the public about the dangers of smoking.

Generally speaking, our intuition does not relent when it comes to something important. If we ignore one intuitive experience, we are likely to have another that may well be more direct. It's as if our intuition refuses to be ignored.

Again, we can find an example of this in the world of business. Once more, understandably, our business executive remains nameless. Excited by a huge franchise deal, he refused to listen to his intuition: the cold sweats, the tell-tale dreams and the sleepless nights. Indeed, despite his gut feelings telling him to back out of the proposed contract, he still signed on the dotted line and went on to lose a massive amount of money. As he said afterwards, 'I failed to listen to my intuition though I was clearly warned that all was not well.'

Remember! We have the creative power within us to make all of our dreams come true; just use our own power. Negative self-judgements act like poison.

We must take the initiative. Understanding our decisions and how they align with our life's principles are the primary factors affecting the way we live.

As well, we must take responsibility for our choices and their consequences. We have to be what we want, and then we can have it. In other words, we have to imagine what it is like to be prosperous before we achieve great wealth. That type of feeling finally draws, from the boundaries of the universe, circumstances and events that will enable us to fulfil our desires.

To fulfil our desires more quickly:

1. We have to ask our higher self, which is part of the limitless consciousness of the universe for whatever we desire.
   Asking for what we want magnifies the power of our imagination, enabling us to achieve what we most desire in life. Every day, we have to keep this type of question firmly in our mind, until it becomes reality and be precise. It is not difficult for our desire then to be fulfilled. This is because our request is answered without any real effort; in other words the vast consciousness of the universe will have already responded to our desire.

2. This consciousness answers and its energy becomes at one with our desire immediately. This part of the process isn't as a result of any direct effort by us at all. By imagining what we want, we anticipate with pleasure the day to come, during which we will fulfil our desire.

3. We must remember to be in tune with what we desire. Indeed, it is perfectly natural to be in agreement with our desire. Worrying about any potential snag or difficulty leaves us disorientated. We simply need to be thankful for what we are about to receive. The more we feel gratitude, the happier we will be. Therefore, we can enjoy the thought of owning our desired possession and allow ourselves to pursue a course of actions inspired by our unconscious mind in tune with the universe.

    'When you want something, the entire universe conspires in helping you to achieve it.' – Paulo Coelho, lyricist and novelist. (See also Chapter 20.)

All too often, we are content to change as little as possible in our lives. In short, our ambitions are limited. However, some of the realities we desire just cannot manifest themselves unless there is a deep change and profound growth in our mind.

In other words, our desires are pathways for growth. We need to allow ourselves to be 'transformed' from within. Only then can we experience success in every way possible.

Remember!

Positive thoughts make us an optimist and negative ones a pessimist.

Stop worrying! Focus on what we want, instead of what we **_don't_** want.

Be positive! Believe anything is possible.

By focusing on the here and now, we improve the quality of our life.

Our unconscious mind brings us **the people, situations and circumstances** to help us succeed.

Life is exactly how we picture it to be. That's why, if we want to change our life, first of all, we have to be aware that any **positive change always comes from within us as a thought.**

Thoughts inspired by love will produce miracles in our life. Thoughts stimulated by fear will have devastating consequences.

We have to imagine what it is like to be prosperous before we achieve great wealth.

9

Belief

To believe means to consider, trust, to accept as true, in other words, to have faith. At the same time, those thoughts which constitute our beliefs are spontaneous. All this allows a belief to be many things: a single thought, a series of judgements, a set of principles and the values which guide our daily life. We trust our beliefs, because they spring from our hidden, unconscious perceptions or convictions. However, the creative power we all possess is only activated when we believe; nothing happens until there is that belief. In other words, to succeed, we must first of all tell ourselves that we WILL succeed.

Therefore, the way we live is built around beliefs. For example, those who believe in themselves can help us all, because they know how we have to have self-belief, a sense of certainty, knowing they can achieve their goals. They are our exemplars. As well, their confidence in us can make us succeed. Their success becomes our success and all this stems from their original self-belief.

Remember, **we see the world not as it is but as we are.** We can only know something for sure through experience. Beliefs affect every aspect of our life. Beliefs act as powerful filters that shape our experience and determine our behaviour as well our physical well-being. Changing our beliefs will also physically affect the world around us. At the same time, we should not judge a situation by its results, but according to our own beliefs. It is, therefore, self-evidently important that our beliefs ensure we can reach our goals.

The two different ways we can live our life

Unconsciously: We observe nature and construct our beliefs according to what we see in this natural world. This is how we are usually educated.

We are told that there is a universe out there and this universe shapes our reality. All this is confirmed for us in our everyday lives. This belief imprints itself on our consciousness each day. Although we are born into this world with no sense of what we can achieve, bit by bit, life starts to teach us to limit our ambitions.

Meanwhile, as adults, we are not even aware that life is built around this belief. Yet it affects us profoundly every moment of our lives. The problem is that this attitude of mind allows us to believe we are not responsible for anything that happens in our lives – that we cannot change the way we live.

Consciously: This is the complete opposite of the unconscious mode. By deciding what we want to believe, we can find the evidence to support this belief in the world around us. Does this sound strange? Maybe yes, maybe no: perhaps our consciousness has already acquired this new way of thinking. The moment we gain a new set of thoughts, i.e. a belief, it becomes a composite part of the consciousness as an exclusive and invisible outline and the same will manifest itself in our life.

We are responsible for what happens to us. We create the life we want. Either we are conscious of being our own life's creator or we are not. Therefore we have to understand how powerful this choice is. When we live our life as the master of our beliefs we can handle anything, because we ultimately know that we have created it. History is replete with famous people whose beliefs enabled them to accomplish remarkable things. Nelson Mandela struggled for most of his adult life against the Apartheid system in South Africa, willing to suffer because of his passionate belief in equality and freedom.

Believing is seeing, or Be-living, with passion and love. As the lecturer, and poet Ralph Waldo Emerson, leader of the Transcendentalist movement of the mid-19th century tells us, 'We are always getting ready to live but never living.' That is why what we believe is what we become. If we want to have self-respect, enjoy life, find fulfilment, then we must earnestly believe we can create these realities for ourselves. If we feel negative about a person, a particular situation or even about ourselves, those downbeat attitudes will harm our prospects. It is important to stop and take time to analyse our beliefs. Are they helping or hindering? Do they move us forward or hold us back?

Interestingly, the roots of the word *belief* comes from *be* and *lief. Be* – being that which exists. The second syllable *lief* can be traced back to the Indo-European word *leubh* the origin of the word – *love*. Together they tell us that *belief* means *to be in a state of love*. The universe gives us the experiences that come from our vision. Belief is a thought repeated again and again and accepted as true and is accepted by our unconscious to such a degree, it shapes our experiences.

Einstein's Law of Vibration states that it is a law of nature that 'nothing rests; everything moves; everything vibrates.' Thus, everything is interconnected. Thoughts are also vibrations and so can provide us with whatever we want or need; the only prerequisite is that we have to believe that this can happen. Any powerful, emotional belief can become a physical reality.

Once we have decided what we want to change in our life, **we have to believe that what we want more than anything actually exists.** Our thoughts, when directed towards a certain objective, will bring that thing to us. But the reverse also occurs if we worry about failure instead. This kind of attitude will result in our goals in life being even further out of reach. This is why belief is so critical.

'A thought, even when false, can affect us if we believe it to be true.' – Mark Fisher, author.

This is why our beliefs determine the limits of what we can achieve. For example, if we have '*I can't*' type of thoughts, being convinced that failure is inevitable. Then the nightmare of failure will come true. By being positive, thinking to ourselves, 'I know I can,' we can accomplish anything we want.

'If you believe you can or if you believe you can't, you are right.' – Henry Ford, industrialist, the founder of the Ford Motor Company.

The only thing that can ever hold us back is our own limiting beliefs. A limiting belief is a one that contradicts our desire. We just picked them up as we bumbled through life and now we drag them behind us everywhere we go. However, 99.99% of our creation is complete before we see ANY physical evidence of it. When we really believe in our desires, then they come true. When we only hope for the best, then what we desire can come true but far more slowly. When our desires are plagued with doubt, then whatever happens in a positive sense happens so slowly, we might as well think about something else.

So, by believing in ourselves, we let life give us the blessings we deserve. **The Creator needs a person who believes so that success can come about.** Of course, we might not always be able to see a way forward straight away. That does not mean there is no way forward. The Creator has at his command all the ways possible. Therefore, we mustn't be discouraged by the size of the task ahead of us. When we believe, the Creator has taken care of it.

'Believe in yourself and all that you are. Know that there is something inside you that is greater than any obstacle. The future belongs to those who believe in the beauty of their own dreams.' – Franklin D Roosevelt, 32nd President of the United States.

The Creator of the universe is fighting for us, arranging things in our favour, ensuring the right people can help us.

The Creator is working in his mysterious way on our behalf. What we desire is coming. Its arrival is only a matter of time. We have to focus on what we desire. The Creator will in time ensure our success, whether it is in the field of work, our physical or mental well-being or whatever we long for. All we have to do is believe. Our beliefs supersede any natural laws. **If all of this takes longer than we expect to happen, then it is simply the case that the Creator is planning for better things for us.** Our job is to not know how. We simply need to believe in these powers and trust in the universe. The Creator will figure out the rest.

Belief is one of the most powerful instruments to shape our reality. It is so powerful that it can shift mass consciousness and can lead to profound changes in our society. **It even has the power to shift the collective consciousness of the whole of civilisation.** Let's think for one moment, how Martin Luther King helped to defeat the evil of segregation in the southern States of America through the power of belief. Overcoming centuries of racial prejudice, he shifted the collective consciousness of an entire nation.

It is the power of our beliefs that attract events, experiences and people in our life to match our beliefs. For this reason, it is crucial to adopt only the beliefs that serve us and to let go of those beliefs that limit us.

Many of our beliefs are taken from our parents, the schools we attended and our friends and acquaintances, as well as the mass media: a collection of innumerable negative inner voices. One thing we can say for sure: that little inner self-critical voice wasn't ours originally. It may seem to be ours, but it isn't really. We have to tell ourselves: '**This is not my true voice.**' It's vital to challenge these nagging doubts or simply to ignore them.

We can either accept these beliefs or reject them. In fact, it is even more important to understand how we believe, than recognise what our belief is. If we hold a belief that we 'know' to be true, as compared with merely assuming it to be true, we have assigned that belief the highest level of trustworthiness.

Change our beliefs as regards money

As we have already learnt, our beliefs are the most important reason why our life is the way it is. That's why we should reject our old negative attitudes towards money and replace them with new positive beliefs. These new beliefs give us what we really want. Let's think: how it feels to be a millionaire, to give to others, to buy something without having to look at the price, to have more money than we can spend?

Whenever we catch ourselves being negative about money, we must stop doing so. Instead, we need to remember how we can think positively about money and concentrate on that belief. Indeed, whatever negative belief we have about ourselves, we must replace it with something positive. That means we identify the negative belief that we want to change. It's good to make detailed notes about our fears. Better still, we should be as precise as possible! For example, it might be that we lack confidence in our ability to sing. Is this because we are shy or lack contacts with whom we could make music? We ought to consider how we would feel if we became the type of singer we would love to be. What are our dreams of success? One way forward is to write down a statement that reflects what we want to become. For example, it could be something like, 'I will acquire all the necessary skills I need to improve my singing. I am giving my best and can already feel like a star performer.' This can be our mantra; by saying it often, it will soon be engrained in our mind as an unconscious belief. The more we do this, the more we will train our mind to think in a new way, a way that leads to a thriving and prosperous life.

How belief revolutionised sport and health

Sport

Fortunately, we keep on breaking free of old beliefs. In 1952, the British athlete Roger Bannister decided that he would set a new world record for running a mile in under four minutes. No one had ever run a mile in such a short time. To many, it seemed impossible. However, on the 6th of May 1954, Roger Bannister completed the mile in 3 minutes 59 seconds. The previous record of 4 minutes 0.1 seconds had stood for nine years.

But Bannister set more than a world record. He also enabled eventually thousands of others to do the same. Indeed, just 46 days after Bannister's success, another runner, John Landy of Australia, ran the mile in 3 minutes and 58 seconds. Nowadays, it is not unknown for even senior students still at school to complete a sub-four minute mile. Roger Bannister showed the world what was possible; he changed for the better the beliefs of literally thousands, inspired by his incredible achievement.

This is why we shouldn't dismiss anything as being impossible. Imaginary boundaries exist in the mind. To accomplish anything, we actually have to believe it is possible. It's simply a question of attitude.

Health

Doctors are still often astounded by how belief can improve a patient's health. For example, in the summer of 1994, a surgeon called J. Bruce

Moseley conducted an amazing experiment on the 'placebo effect'. A placebo is in appearance a 'real' medical treatment, but in reality isn't.

Doctors had long been aware of this 'placebo effect' – the idea that we can give a patient a fake medicine which the patient believes to be real, that in turn, will bring about some sort of recovery. Studies have even shown that placebos can have a positive effect on conditions such as depression, chronic pain and insomnia.

Research on the placebo effect has focused on the relationship of the mind and body. One of the most common theories in this regard is that the placebo effect is due to a person's expectations. If a patient believes he/she can be helped by the supposed treatment, then it's possible that the body's own metabolism can replicate the benefits of the actual medication.

Here is an example that relates to both the placebo affect and the impact of having belief in others positive mental attitude. On an extremely hot June afternoon in1972, an incident occurred that became the catalyst, which eventually encouraged me to set up the charity, the Uspar Trust mentioned in the Preface, to help the poor and deprived in my home town in Kashmir.

I was passing by a doctor's surgery and saw a local man, a tailor, stood outside. He was holding his baby son, who was around one year old. I asked him what was wrong and he told me that his son was sick, but that he couldn't afford the doctor's fees or the prescription. The poor tailor was totally nonplussed. The doctor had said to him that there was nothing he could do as the child was so dehydrated and anyway the father could not afford the prescription. The doctor's words 'Go home! Your son may live, maybe not,' were still ringing in his ears. He had no idea what to do.

However, he knew I was a student and had moved to the UK. In desperation, he asked me to look at his son, thinking I was a doctor. So, I pretended to check the little boy's pulse and then said, 'He will be fine.' Instantly, the father's facial expression changed with this ray of hope, as if I were an angel.

Of course, I felt very disturbed by what had happened and didn't want to raise any false hopes and so went to see the doctor. The doctor told me that the baby was badly dehydrated and needed among other things a drip and to stay in an air-conditioned room. Immediately, I paid for the fees and the prescription, before taking the man and his baby to the hotel next door, where I booked a room for them. Quickly, I obtained the medication, administered it to the baby and the next day he was fine.

Remember!

Our creative power is only activated when we believe; nothing happens until we believe.

Try to banish any concerns or doubts from our mind, because once we believe something to be true, whether it is or not, we will then act as if it is.

Imaginary boundaries exist in the mind. If we CAN believe, the mind can achieve. We can only accomplish whatever we actually believe is possible.

Our beliefs will dictate how we act. If we believe in a cause, we fight for it. If we believe in others, they can achieve great things.

When we live our life as the master of our beliefs we can handle anything, because we ultimately know that we have created the circumstances we find ourselves in.

The power of each belief comes only from the individual believer. That means we can believe whatever we want to believe. As long as we believe it to be true, it will be true for us.

Beliefs create perceptions that affect our self-esteem, relationships, prospects and even our health. Either we accept those beliefs unquestioningly, or we evaluate them and work out which to maintain and which to reject.

A strong *belief* is as effective as a strong wish. We believe in our ultimate success and pay no attention to little setbacks, stumbles and slips and thereby set in operation the strongest forces known in the world of thought.

The Creator of the universe is fighting on our behalf, arranging things in our favour, ensuring that we can fulfil our dreams.

10
Imagination

'Imagination rules the world.' – Napoleon, French Emperor.

We are all incredibly resourceful and amazingly creative, because we can imagine. There are no boundaries when we exercise our ability to imagine. At the same time, what we perceive in our mind's eye is the first step towards changing our lives. Whatever we can imagine can become real. **It is as if these imagined thoughts become the precursor to our future successes.** Imagine what life would be like if the mind could always be focused on thoughts that were filled with joy, peace, love, abundance and success!

We have to be happy and excited in anticipation of what is coming because it is certain that what we want already exists. We are like a powerful magnet. What we feel at any time is what we attract to ourselves. Therefore, if we feel there is no escape for us from the poverty we are trapped in, then we will never be able to do so. (We have to feel rich instead!) Similarly, if we feel we can't lose weight, then we won't lose weight. When we feel sick, we cannot recover, until we imagine ourselves to be well again – otherwise, it defies the law of 'like attracts like'.

Anything we want to create, first of all, we must imagine it and then believe it. Enjoying the thought of it, makes our wishes come true. This kind of positive energy is contagious. When we appreciate the good life other people have, this feeling, in turn, encourages them and consequently also improves our own prospects.

On the other hand, disapproval and envy are also infectious and cause gloom and misery. Therefore, the appreciation of the success of others, a feeling of joy and the manifestation of hope are clear signs that we are about to achieve our goals. As well, in this way, they will come about more quickly.

Remember! We can magnify the power of any mental picture tenfold or by even more, just by connecting it to real emotions. Always attach an emotion to each image, i.e. imagine how we are going to feel as soon as we will have fulfilled our ambitions.

Positive, high-vibration thoughts are like multifaceted magnets attracting people, circumstances and opportunities back to us. The universe literally helps. Of course, our vibrations go up and down with our moods through the day. We can still make progress even when our vibrations are low; when we feel bored or depressed, for example. However, to succeed is far more difficult in this type of situation. To attain our objectives far more swiftly and easily, we need our vibrations to be high, by feeling joyful and excited. These high vibrations bring us even more happiness, love, and fulfilment into our life. Examples of high vibration thoughts are:

1. I love my life.
2. I have everything I need.
3. I have all the love I deserve and desire.
4. I am healthy and full of energy and vitality.

We must picture in our mind's eye, what we desire! This will inspire us to take action. An 'inspired action' feels like that we're enjoying the process. We get a lot of bangs for our bucks. This is like a guidance system which operates beyond our imagination, yet exists within us right now. Indeed, it is something we may trust above all else.

As we already said, but it cannot be emphasised enough, emotions help magnify our ability to make our desires become reality. When imagining the life we want, feel the joy, happiness and excitement of the situation. The stronger these emotions are, the faster we can make real what we want. We mustn't forget, however, our emotions are the slaves of our thoughts, and we ourselves are a slave to our emotions. Therefore, when we direct our thoughts properly, we can also control our emotions. Controlling our emotions doesn't mean ignoring or repressing them. Instead it means learning to process them and respond to them in healthy, helpful ways. For example, if we feel ourselves start to lose control, we must deliberately take a step back from what's going on. That means we imagine what's happening is happening to someone else. What advice would we give to that person?

To enhance the emotions controlled by our imagination, we have to build up the feeling of ALREADY having succeeded. In other words, when we see our dream home, we mustn't think of it as something that COULD come to us in the future. For example, it's far more effective to imagine we have our dream home RIGHT NOW! Through our powers of imagination, we think how we would feel if we were in that home THIS INSTANT, NOT at some undetermined time in the future.

When we draw on our imagination to be creative, by using the five senses (sound, sight, taste, touch and smell) we make the image real. There are also five inner senses: imagination, as well as insight, instinct, inspiration and intuition. These other four senses empower the imagination.

'Take time to imagine. Imagination opens doors to original thought. Imagination lifts you above the mundane nuts and bolts of daily pressures. It gives you a glimpse into the "promised land," a moment of clarity and understanding not easily achieved by travelling the more commonly used pathways of logic, strategy and tactics.' – Robert Wilson, artist and writer.

Similarly, Albert Einstein, the amazingly brilliant physicist, whose original insights completely rewrote the laws of science, commented, 'Logic will get you from A to Z; imagination will get you everywhere.'

Through our emotions we can create and also see the others enjoying the benefits of our creativity. By instilling our imagination with emotion, we speed up the process by which our desires materialise into reality. Another way to boost the emotions we feel within our creative imagination is to imagine that it is not just us alone benefiting from our success. Staying with the analogy of wishing to buy a new house, we can envisage our children having fun playing in the garden, and visualise our spouse loving the brand new living room, or indeed, think of our family and friends visiting, experiencing a warm welcome to our new home.

To make our imagination more powerful consider the following examples:

A. Want a new car? Our desire to do so may be strong at first, but for many of us such feelings soon wane. To retain the thought of the new car, buy something as a reminder: a fancy air freshener, driving gloves or a set of car keys. These simple reminders help keep the thought of the new vehicle completely fresh in our mind.

B. Take some time every day, morning and/or night time before going to bed to relax. Breathe slowly and deeply. We will enter into the *theta* state of mind. (See Chapter 5.) By creating in our minds a picture of ourselves in the future, a picture that pleases us, an image that is so attractive, we cannot stop thinking about it. While doing so, we will understand that time and space are moving towards our ideal. By establishing clearly in our mind this powerful impression, it will seem so real to us that it will inspire us to take the necessary steps to make such an image reality.

C. Another way to achieve a theta state of mind is again to sit comfortably, relax, and breathe slowly and deeply. Then we imagine watching an empty giant screen. We start to create a movie in our mind and see ourselves achieving what we want. It's better to make the image big, bright and bold. Once we can see it clearly, we put ourselves in the movie – as if we were reliving a memory. We are the star of our own film, while as much as possible bringing into play our five senses.

D. We have to see ourselves doing the things we need to do in order to reach our goal. As well, we shouldn't just see it – but also feel it! We will then go on to believe in it! In this way, we will make it happen. This allows us to imagine what it will be like when our goal has in fact materialised. We ensure that we assume ownership of our goal. For example, we can picture being stood on a stage knowing that we have won first place and our name is about to be announced to the audience. We then feel the rush of emotions, as if it were actually happening to us. In essence, what we are doing is creating the pattern in spirit of what we want to attain in reality. When we've finished visualising our success, then we can say to ourselves something like, 'Thanks for doing so well!'

If we can't imagine something so vividly for some reason, just think of any sound, smell or image which can be associated with whatever we want. What we are really trying to do is engage our emotions, when we imagine our desired goal. Our feelings, allied to the five senses, are the fuel which fires up our imagination.

This imaginative process is so powerful, if we do this for thirty days amazing things will start to happen. If we have any lingering doubts discard them. We do this by saying, 'I have no doubts. I know I can succeed.'

E. Everything starts by being imagined. So, first of all, we have to imagine the desired outcome in our mind and act as if it is already reality. All this starts with a picture, before the picture becomes real. It all happens by that same law of *like attracts like*. It takes time to build up the perfect image. We need to focus on it daily. We can do the following: Paint the image in the mind or recreate the image with words on a sheet of paper; write out what is desired again and again. We picture ourselves in different scenarios enjoying our life as a result of this success. By so doing, we are depositing this image in the treasure chest of our unconscious mind. When that happens, success will come about, because we are making part of our own reality.We can create an experience through sheer pretence. The human nervous system can't distinguish between actual experience and one imagined vividly. So the rules are simple: imagine success; imagining the sort of person we want to become; acting as if we have already succeeded.

In addition,

a. Sincerely forgive others, as well as forgive ourselves for all the past mistakes that have been made. When we forgive ourselves we unlock the door of our true self, where all the dimensions of creativity are. See Chapter 14.

b. Visualise the amazing qualities we already possess.

c. Don't worry about what other people do. Do everything at our own pace.

    d. Improve personal appearance so that we look as if we belong to the community we wish to join.

    e. Be surrounded by people already doing what we want to do. Find a mentor, if possible.

The concept *fake it till you make it* serves as a way to build confidence, prevent negative thoughts and instil new, more positive habits. It implicitly forces us into action, to do something we wouldn't otherwise do. Eventually, we will come to enjoy this type of activity or at the very least, dislike it less.

F. Before an event, athletes create mental images of the exact movements they want to emulate during the competition. This skill substantially increases the effectiveness of their performance. It is called *creating positive coincidences*. People all around the world have experienced this in their own lives and will say that our world can be shaped by our thoughts and beliefs. We have to act as if we are winners. That's why we need to rehearse the future we want in our mind's eye. We must keep focused on our chosen prize and believe in it to our very core. Then everything will work itself out for the best.

G. This is a true incident that shows how the powerful our imagination can be in reality:

One afternoon I visited my younger sister, Nahid. I was sitting in her front lounge with her husband and two sons and drinking tea. She interrupted the normal family chit chat and told me that she had bought a rather large sofa. Despite all their efforts, they couldn't get it into the lounge. I didn't know what to say, and so said nothing. However, I was intrigued by this simple conundrum and, therefore, before I left, I decided to apply my knowledge on the *'power of the imagination'*. I asked my sister to point out the exact place where she would like to place the sofa.

She moved a few steps and stopped on the spot where she intended to put the sofa and said, 'Here, in this place.'

I replied, 'Just imagine right now that your new sofa is already in the place you have just pointed out and we are both sitting on it.'

She said, 'How is that possible?'

I replied, 'Well! Leave the "how" for later on. That doesn't matter for the moment.'

I left her feeling rather confused, but I promised to call back the next day.

After I had left my sister's house, things began to happen. Within a few hours, the family had managed to place the sofa exactly where my sister had wanted it to go.

The next day, when I arrived at the house, I was greeted by a wonderful smile from Nahid.

Remember!

'Imagination will often carry us to worlds that never were. But without it we go nowhere.' – Carl Sagan, astronomer.

When we really imagine something we really want with real sense of emotional commitment, then it is likely to happen.

Positive thinking attracts good things and to get what we want we just have to imagine it: when we think about what we want, and we emit that frequency, we cause the energy of what we want to vibrate at that frequency and we bring it to ourselves.

Imagine what we desire. Our five senses are the real gateways to our imagination.

Imagination is the beginning of creation.

Anything we want to create, first rehearse it in our mind, as if we are practising it again and again. We have probably heard the old joke about Carnegie Hall in New York, one of the world's top concert venues for classical music. One day, a tourist asks a cab driver how to get to Carnegie Hall, to which the cab driver replies: 'Practise, practise, practise!'

We can magnify the power of any mental picture ten times or more just by connecting the image with real emotions.

Positive, high vibration thoughts are like magnets, which will attract people, circumstances and opportunities with the same positive high vibrations to us.

When, for example, we see our dream home, picture ourselves there. Feel the joy and happiness we would get by looking at the garden, the building itself, the high quality of the indoor decor, etc.

11
The Need to Focus

By focusing, by concentrating on those thoughts and images of our express desires, we determine our own reality. To focus in this way is both an act of will and of supreme importance. What we focus on is what we achieve. The success of anything we do begins by focusing on what we want.

Often, the degree to which our life lacks success depends on how much or how little we focus on what we aspire to. When we are not fully focused on what we yearn for, our goals in life recede further into the distance – something we will not even notice. Being too concerned about less important things means we fail to focus on our main concerns. For example, being penny wise, pound foolish, or preferring quantity to quality.

> 'When you focus on problems you have more problems, when you focus on possibilities you will have more opportunities.' – Zig Ziglar, author and motivational speaker.

Whatever we want, focus on that. There's enough for everybody in this world: food, money, love and anything else we care to mention. Unfortunately, not everyone gets their fair share. We don't have to be one of the unlucky ones. We mustn't simply give in and say to ourselves, 'I don't know what to do.' This attitude creates more confusion in the mind. Therefore, **we must focus on personal growth and success.** When we focus on our problems, they loom ever larger and distract us more and more. The solution is to treat our problems as challenges, dealing with them one by one. A good idea is to write down a set of priorities: the most urgent first, the least important last, and the rest somewhere in between. This often means we have to begin with the hardest task first. Lloyd Blankfein, the CEO of Goldman Sachs, once said that the first thing he does in the office each day is the task he dreads the most. Whatever we don't want to do, we must do first. This then eliminates that nagging feeling which saps our energy while we try to postpone the inevitable.

Simply thinking about a problem can mean we don't focus on any potential solution. One way forward is, first of all, to focus on our blessings. By so doing, we open up our heart to more success.

We must be able to focus clearly on our purpose in life and picture everything in full detail. Here, the power of the mind is the key. By keeping focused on them, our desires become stronger, becoming aligned with our dreams.

Remember, to focus successfully, we have to think deeply about what we want to do. Of course, we can, if we wish, make a set of notes. Everything will come good, as the Creator reveals his secrets in all due course. The power of such thoughts attracts what we want. Every thought has a vibrating energy pattern that will resonate with similar objects and events that already exist or are coming into existence.

'Where focus goes, energy flows.' – Tony Robbins, motivational speaker, life coach and self-help author.

Every single second, the brain absorbs an incredible amount of information; 11 million pieces of information per second to be exact. We actually pay attention to about 40 of them, which is still a lot, particularly if we're trying to complete or even start a task, according to Dr Joseph Cardillo, lecturer, author and inspirational speaker.

Dr Lucy Jo Palladino, author and psychologist, recommends that if the mind is wandering, a quick walk outdoors is an effective short break. Take 'some deep breaths while focused on a beautiful object, preferably of nature e.g. a plant, a flower'. Moreover, breathing slowly and deeply through the nose and exhaling through either the nose or mouth, helps us to relax and lowers stress levels and reduce feelings of anxiety and any related symptoms. As well, to make sure we do improve our powers of concentration, get enough sleep on a regular basis.

We always consciously choose what we want to focus on. We use our conscious mind to create what we want by focusing on it. Focusing on the negative means we disregard the positive. When making such a choice, we send a signal to our unconscious mind which compares this with all our other experiences in life, to see which of our emotions is associated with that particular thought. For example, if we say 'I feel wealthy' – but in our unconscious mind we feel that all rich people are gangsters – then we are not going to become wealthy. On the other hand, if in our unconscious mind we welcome the idea of prosperity, we are protecting ourselves from failure. Our attitudes are the seeds which will grow our future self.

> 'The greatest discovery of my generation is that a human being can alter his life by altering his attitudes.' – William James, philosopher and psychologist.

When we say yes to something, we attract more of the same into our life, because that is what we are focused on. The simple effort of looking for something positive will inspire us. As a result of all this, we will begin immediately to attract those circumstances which please us the most.

That's why, if we want to have a set of happy relationships, we must focus on one right thing we can do to improve them. For example, it's far more positive to concentrate on our friends' finer qualities. If we want to shed 20 pounds in weight, we must focus on losing one pound at first, then the next, and the one after that.

One smile can start a friendship. One word can end a fight. One look can save a relationship. One person can change our lives. We shouldn't underestimate these kinds of small steps, because they can mean everything. Small steps can lead to big changes. In other words, **if we can't do great things, do small things in a great way.**

When we pay attention to anything, we are using our powers of concentration. We have to focus in such a way so that we get rid of our old, negative thoughts. This in turn activates a harmonious condition for the fulfillment of our desires.

> 'The secret of change is to focus all of your energy, not on fighting the old, but on building the new.' – Socrates, philosopher.

In addition, the key to making boring tasks more interesting is to think of ways we can psych ourselves up, by making a list of options.

Examples include playing upbeat music, opening a window or by varying the tasks in question. Alternatively, to motivate ourselves, we can try practising self-talk. As Dr Lucy Jo Palladino advises, we can say to ourselves: 'What do I need to do now? Stay with it; stay with it; stay with it,' or, 'I've finished things that are harder than this.'

Furthermore, we can add,

> 'If you're super stressed or anxious, you need ways to calm down. Make a list of soothing strategies, such as playing relaxing music, breathing deeply or sipping herbal tea.' – Lucy Jo Palladino.

What we have just read explains why we should focus in a clear and positive manner on a daily basis on what we want. Doing so will keep our desires strong and vibrant, in other words, feeling happy at the thought of what is going to happen to us.

> 'Know that it is absolute that what you want is done. What you seek is seeking you.' – Rumi, poet, jurist, Islamic scholar and Sufi mystic.

Remember!

The way we focus is like a lens through which we perceive reality. Make sure we focus in a clear and positive direction.

We can all focus on something when we want to. However, our ability to do so can be strengthened through meditation and other mental exercises. Practice may not make it perfect, but it can be at least good enough.

When we try to do too much, we end up doing nothing. To avoid making this mistake, focus on the immediate. This requires making a conscious choice, clarity of purpose, and real commitment.

Remember this means we must focus *in the moment*. We have already explained this means being *mindful* i.e. we need to be more conscious of life as it happens. For example, every time we find our mind wandering elsewhere, tell ourselves, 'Be here now,' until we finally get used to doing it. See Chapter 15.

We need a vision. Focus on it with all our energy. Otherwise our energy will be scattered and therefore wasted.

The ideal time to focus is in the morning or late at night.

The simple effort of looking for any positive aspects of our life will inspire us and will begin immediately to attract those circumstances which please us the most.

12

Intentions

Whatever we intend to do, is an infinite source of our potential. This means that inevitably, our intentions take us in new directions. **As well, whatever we intend to do, we eventually create.**

For anything we want, we just have be determined to do it, doing whatever is required while we remain honest with ourselves and those around us. Therefore, we should always concentrate completely on what we want. This will make our dreams blossom into reality, especially, when we avoid any negative thoughts, and always formulate our intentions in such a way that they reflect the outcome we desire. Expressing our intentions is another way of saying that we can conceive something wonderful in our lives. Remember that the Creator can generate infinite possibilities through our intentions. We are a magical being but may not realise this. Kahlil Gibran, author of *The Prophet*, states, 'The appearance of things changes according to your emotions and thus we see the magic in them, while the magic and beauty are really in ourselves.' When we acknowledge this in ourselves, we will see magic in our everyday lives.

We must ensure that our intentions are clear and they must be with the best of motives. When we decide on what we do, we have to be clear and precise, before asking the universe to fulfil our desires. However, we must be careful! Remember the old saying, **'Be careful what you wish for – it may come true!'**

We must pay attention to anything that affects our personal feelings, after we have formulated exactly our intentions. Our body will follow our mind's commands (i.e. our intentions) and we will begin to follow the path to success. Our mind may become confused and so we say to ourselves, 'No way will I ever achieve what I want,' or something like, 'This is impossible!' If such thoughts enter our mind, we must re-express our intentions, so that they feel realistic and attainable. Sometimes it helps to divide up an important intention into a set of smaller constituent parts. For example: 'In ten days, I will have x pounds,' is an intention that will not work for the overwhelming majority of people. However, an intention such as, 'In the next few months, I will be earning more,' may come true sooner than we think.

These kinds of intentions are goals, which can empower us all. By accepting full responsibility for our present circumstances, we can fully understand how we take charge of our own circumstances at any time and act appropriately. As Steve Maraboli, author and life-changing speaker, tells us, 'Take action! An inch of movement will bring you closer to your goals than a mile of intention.'

Remember, if our intentions are fully visualised and sustained with positive self-belief, they are made far more potent.

With every intention, there is another act of creation. If we say we can't afford to buy what we desire because we don't have enough money, we are telling the universe in fact that we don't have any money. The universe hears and obeys us on the basis of 'Your wish is my command'. In other words, we get what we wish for. We are allowing poverty into our lives and that is why we will remain poor.

To become more prosperous, we simply must intend it! Therefore, we have to think about what we want, not what we don't want or can't have. If we desire financial success, we make that our intention in life.

To realise our intentions, it's important to understand three powerful forces: Desire, Belief, and Expectation. Before anything that we want to happen, can happen, we have to have wanted it to happen. We have to believe that it will happen and we must expect it to happen.

Well! It did work for me. Although I had a post graduate degree in commerce (B Com Hon's), yet in 2002 I intended to study for Law Degree. My son commented, 'Dad you are in your fifties, you're too old now!' I ignored his comment and sought guidance from Leeds Metropolitan University. I was advised to seek permission from the Law Society. I received a positive reply. Subsequently, I successfully completed the two years part-time course in 2004. My family only knew about it when they were apparently attending someone else's degree ceremony!

Remember!

Intentions take us in new directions. Without clear intentions, we simply drift through life.

In order to escape from the mediocre and find the extraordinary in our lives, we have to decide on what our intentions must be. Therefore, we have to ask the Creator what it is we should desire.

Whichever intention we choose, the mind is directing our inner energy in the right direction. Events will then fall into place to make that intention come true.

When we become clear that we have a *purpose*, it becomes our guide.

Our intentions are at their most powerful when they come from our heart, because then they are directly fuelled by the passion of our spiritual truth, the reason we were born.

When we lack any real purpose in life, the result is confusion – confusion which we create for ourselves and confusion which we allow others to create for us. We become a passive victim and experience a life beset by random events, over which we have no control.

13
Gratitude

Gratitude is both an expression of appreciation for an act of kindness and also a state of mind. By being grateful, we can count our blessings every day, indeed, in every minute of our lives. This leads on to being mindful, possessing a moment-by-moment awareness of our thoughts, feelings, physical sensations and the world we live in.

By focusing on the abundance we can find in our lives, we discover a greater capacity for generosity, as well as contentment. As well, by expressing our gratitude, we acquire a rewarding habit that affirms the grace of the benefactor. Gratitude opens up our hearts, encourages us to savour each gift that comes our way and frees us from jealously guarding our possessions. It lets us celebrate today rather than passively waiting for some other, ill-defined future achievement. It is a reminder that one can *always* find reason to be glad.

> 'Gratitude is not only the greatest of virtues, but the parent of all the others' – Marcus Tullius Cicero, a writer, speaker, philosopher and politician.

When someone gives us a gift or passes a compliment, we reply with a word or two of thanks. By doing this, we are telling our benefactor, as well as the universe itself, that we are allowing ourselves to receive the gift. 'Let us be grateful to people who make us happy; they are the charming gardeners who make our souls blossom,' wrote Marcel Proust, French novelist. We need to do this with everything in life that we want to receive. Of course, if we don't want something, we politely refuse. However, be careful. Whatever we have declined, e.g. a present or an offer of help, may well prove to be useful later on. So let's think about anything like this carefully, before we say 'no'.

If we feel grateful for every small thing we already have, then we will find more things to be grateful for. Therefore, be thankful as often as possible, or what we already have. We should be grateful for whatever blessings, accomplishments, dreams and ambitions, we possess. It's crucial to bear all these advantages in mind, by analysing our own talents and abilities, our strengths and achievements and by being delighted in how well we've accomplished something, no matter how trivial that particular success may seem to be.

For example, a few years ago, I attended an introductory course on life coaching. During the first tea break, I met a couple from Wales who were not happy with some aspects of the course. I felt the same way. We talked a little more and I mentioned my thoughts about the power of suggestion and the role of the unconscious mind in finding true happiness.

Later, the same couple introduced me to another attendee, a lady in her thirties.

I asked this lady what was upsetting her.

She replied that she often felt depressed and felt her life seemed to lack any real purpose. She added, 'I came here to find some answers.'

I got her to talk about herself a little more.

She told me, 'I am happily married, have lovely children, live in a large house and we are reasonably sound financially.'

I replied, 'My dear lady, you don't realise how lucky you are. You have plenty of blessings for which you should be truly grateful.'

She didn't understand what I had said and quickly asked, 'What do you mean?'

I answered, 'Please listen carefully. Many of us often struggle to find the right partner, to have a family or a nice place to live in. Can you count your blessings, including the ones you've already mentioned?'

She replied, 'Oh, I've never thought like this before. I can count many more blessings than problems.'

I added, 'When you go home, twice a day, sit and relax. Think of all of your blessings. The more thankful you are for the blessings you have received, the Creator will let you have even more to be thankful for. Do you understand what I mean?'

She said joyfully, 'Thank you, Mohammed, You've made my day. In fact, I've found the answers I was looking for. I might as well go home straight away!'

For all those things we desire, we have to **be thankful for them** *before* **the event,** as if they already have come into existence before we ask for them, rather than after we have received them. By focusing on what we have and what we feel grateful for, we will then begin to see more of the same. By doing this, we will start to attract more of those things we really will feel grateful for. It is only through this sense of gratitude that will make our life far richer.

Nothing new can come in to our life without this powerful sense of gratitude drawing it towards us. Therefore, gratitude itself is the first step to the path of joy. The more we are able to express gratitude for those small successes in our life, the more positive things will appear in our life. At the same time, when we feel this strong sense of gratitude, the more self-confidence and material success takes the place of fear and doubt.

To begin with, we must express of gratitude for everything we have. This kind of appreciation can create personal wealth, even in the midst of hard times. Failing to value the success of others is a sure way to limit our own personal growth and prosperity. This means that the main key to achievement is to let ourselves be in a continual state of gratitude, while at the same time welcoming and acknowledging other people's accomplishments. Consequently, this is what we should focus each day. We don't even need to worry about when to take action, because when this is how we feel, ideas, one after the other, will flood into our mind, encouraging and energising us, so that we will not hesitate any longer. By entering this positive state of mind, our life-source becomes the focal point of our existence and we can exploit this force to create any outcome we want. Without it, we can achieve nothing. It's like trying to swim against an ocean current. Every time we try to swim a little way forward, the waves just push us back.

In addition, by having our mind suffused with a deep sense of thankfulness, our outlook on life becomes far more often positive, indeed, even joyful, and full of compassion and love. Of course sometimes, we all face moments of despair. Sorrow and grief are an inevitable part of the human condition, but those who are grateful to be alive bounce back quickly. To achieve this state of joy, we have to start thinking about what we have to be thankful for.

Believe me, dear reader; we are bound to have a lot to be thankful for.

Something important:

None of this boosts the ego of some insecure universal consciousness or the Creator. All this works because our frame of mind is now one of joy and expectancy. Focusing on what we have rather than what we don't have means our personal energy creates an impression of success. In return, the universe responds by giving us a lot more. Without this powerful sense of gratitude, the energy we put out is negative and self-defeating, as if to say it's inevitable that, 'I don't have enough.' Through the law of cause and effect, we will keep on losing more and more.

How to Express Gratitude

It's really easy. We can start off by making up short sayings about our power, courage and insight. These statements are 'little truths' about us, our life and the individuals connected to us based upon real experiences and the daily recognition of the success of others. Occasionally when we are busy we lose sight of the great gifts of life. Therefore we need to remind ourselves of all those things we should always be thankful for. If we're already writing down a list of things to be grateful about, we'll soon have lots of positive thoughts. We could simply note things such as, 'I'm resilient,' 'I have a lot of supportive relationships,' or 'The higher power supports me.'

We have to get into the habit of expressing gratitude. It's necessary to spend a few minutes each day doing this, so that we can practise being thankful for what we have. We can write our *gratitude list* and read it (out loud if possible) in the morning, as soon as we wake up, during our morning commute, while in the shower, just before going to bed at night. We'll notice in just a matter of days how long that list becomes and how much our basic attitudes change for the better.

Some Suggestions:

'**I am** so grateful for my good health. I am growing old gracefully.'

'**I am** truly thankful that my family is so wonderful.' (Remember, gratitude is actually a form of love. When we feel gratitude for another, we begin to complement that person and the relationship becomes stronger.)

'**I am** so grateful now that I am earning so much per month. As well, I have a job I love, a successful career and I can afford anything I want for my family or myself.'

In an experiment carried out by Dr Robert Emmons at the University of California-Davis, people who kept a weekly record of things which made them feel grateful enjoyed better physical health, much happier, more optimistic and exercised regularly.

But what if something particularly bad happens? What do we do then?

The solution to anything like this is a technique called 'Energy Redirection Technique' (ERT). This basically means we need to *stay positive*, even in the most trying circumstances. By redirecting our thoughts, we can constantly focus on what our ideal life would be. We imagine seeing ourselves doing those things. Our thoughts are a form of vibrating energy. As we have already been told, that which we focus on, we attract. The problem is that bad things do sometimes happen: accidents, illnesses, a bad break-up, being laid off work. When this happens, if we dwell on the sudden bad situation, we just create negative energy. This makes things even worse and keeps us trapped for much longer.

When we're truly depressed, we shouldn't attempt to apply positive thinking to make the gloom disappear. This sort of positive thinking unavoidably leads to more let-downs as it doesn't provide the motivating power required to support it. Rather, we must accept willingly how we feel, yet remain optimistic – and find our unmet needs that are producing these feelings of depression. We can then discover how to meet those needs in ways which empower us. One solution is to share our feelings of with others, perhaps a trusted friend or a professional counsellor. This enables us to overcome our difficulties, step by step, with patience and determination. We must start along this difficult path as soon as possible.

If one has any doubt that ERT can be accomplished under even the most trying circumstances, one should look at the holocaust survivor Victor Frankl, author of the book *Man's Search for Meaning*. Despite being a prisoner in a Nazi concentration camp, Frankl believes he survived because of his ability to redirect his thoughts and constantly focus on what his ideal life would be. For example, he would see himself teaching classes at university or imagine a far better life outside the concentration camp. At the same time, he watched others marched into the gas chambers.

Frankl states that the main reason that some survived while so many others were killed was that the survivors had a far more positive mental attitude.

'Miracles seldom occur in the lives of those who do not consider them possible. There could be a miracle waiting for you this minute. Please make room for it in your thinking.' – Neale Donald Walsch, author.

While it is easy to be thankful for the good things in life, those who lead the richest lives are always thankful for the setbacks they endure. Life's difficulties are something we can actually be thankful for, because gratitude can turn a negative into a positive. That's why we should be thankful even for our problems. If we are going through a tough time, be grateful for the lessons we are learning, the strength we gain and the compassion we find for others going through their own personal difficulties. Difficult times and difficult people can be our best teachers. They teach us to find peace and harmony within. They build our strength and compassion. When things get really tough, if we want to keep our mental health intact, they can even force us to live in the present moment.

Remember!

If we are grateful for every small thing we already have then we will find more things to be grateful for.

When we feel grateful, our mind becomes far more active. Ideas occur to us in far greater number and much more frequently. We can achieve a life of fulfilment rather than one of emptiness.

By being grateful, we can get through any challenge or hardship. Those who experience a genuine sense of gratitude tend to be more positive, enjoy life more, and feel far more loving and compassionate.

Think of what is good in our life: our strengths – not our weaknesses. Count our blessings. Even be grateful for the times when we have been lucky.

One of the easiest ways to cultivate this powerful sense of gratitude is to keep a journal. Just write in it for five minutes a day. This will make us **focus on the positive aspects of our day, rather than allowing it to be overshadowed by any more negative features of our daily routine.**

14
Forgiveness: Letting go of our Anger

Forgiveness is life-giving. This is because it gives us the opportunity to let go of the past and no longer fear the future. This is empowering. We simply have to think, 'If it does not flow, let it go.' It means, we stop fighting our current state of affairs and moved on with our life. It becomes obvious that we instantly get our peace of mind back. Any fear or distress disappears. This means we forgive the faults and mistakes of others – but, most importantly of all, we must also forgive ourselves for our own slip-ups and blunders. Those of us who find it difficult to forgive ourselves also do not seem to be able to forgive others. Yet those who are closest to us, we do forgive, as we still want them to be a part of our lives.

When we forgive ourselves, we unlock the door to our true self, where all the dimensions of creativity are to be found. If we wish to free those creative impulses, then we must first of all choose to forgive ourselves. This in turn opens up to the possibility of thinking in a new and exciting way, enabling us to become truly successful.

At the same time, it really doesn't matter if the person who hurt us deserves to be forgiven. Forgiveness is a gift we give to ourselves. The act of forgiveness is like a treasure trove, but in a contradictory way, the more it is spent, the more it increases. This is because the act of forgiveness allows us to move on, to discard the barren past of anger and resentment. As Steve Maraboli, author and life-changing speaker, tells us, 'The truth is, unless you let go, unless you forgive yourself, unless you forgive the situation, unless you realise that the situation is over, you cannot move forward... Let go of the things that are weighing you down, from relationships long gone, to old grudges and regrets, to all could haves and should haves. Free yourself from the burden of a past you cannot change. Cry. Forgive. Learn. Move on. Let your tears water the seeds of your future happiness.'

Remember, we are the co-creator of our own world. Our circumstances are not responsible for our parlous state; it is our emotional thinking which creates our personal circumstances. That's why we need to be able to forgive ourselves. Instead, by letting go of all our anger, no longer blaming ourselves or others for failures which can never be rectified, we can stand tall and be proud.

'When you judge another, you do not define them, you define yourself.' – Wayne Dyer, author and motivational speaker.

By letting go of the past in this way, we are allowing ourselves to find is the shortest route to a positive inner transformation. We will know how powerful this new approach is when we start seeing the positive changes in our personality without any effort on our part.

The source of many of our problems, such as feeling stressed, suffering from a deep sense of frustration or fearing something new or challenging, is our inability to let go of past disappointments. To a huge degree, we could rid ourselves of the irritation and stress of our daily lives, by accepting, indeed embracing, the present reality as it is and discarding all those notions of how we wanted things to be. This allows us to enjoy living in the present. That's why we should disregard all of those other possibilities relating to an alternative past or future. It's usually quite hard to let go and move on, but as soon as we bid farewell to those encumbrances, we become liberated and realise it is the best decision we've ever made.

Through the act of forgiveness, it's as if a huge weight is removed from our minds. At the same time, if we may be permitted to mix our metaphors, the door to self-love, in the best sense of this word, is opened. Refusing to forgive keeps that door locked. When we don't forgive, we make ourselves suffer. That is why forgiveness blesses both those who give and those who receive. After all, life is too short to spend at war with ourselves.

Letting go of yesterday's troubles is our first step towards happiness today. If we feel we are sinking under the weight of all of our past disappointments, we must forget about them! As well, we have to let go of those people who drag us down. **Self-evidently, it's always better to surround ourselves with those who bring out the best in us.** One of the most rewarding moments in life is when we finally find the courage to let go of what we can't change. Once more, Steve Marboli, author and life-changing speaker, explains this necessity with absolute clarity: 'Letting go means to come to the realisation that some people are a part of your history, but not a part of your destiny.' Glenn Clark, author, has made the following helpful remark: 'We don't need that negativity in our life. Keep calm and be positive. Good things will happen. If we wish to travel far and fast, travel light, take off all our envies, jealousies, un-forgiveness, selfishness, and fears.'

In other words, we need to let go of wishing others to change, focus on ourselves, change ourselves first and then become a shining example to others. When we change, the world changes with us: this is what 'be the change and see the change' means.

In reality, forgiveness has very little to do with someone else. Forgiveness is the way ahead for the person who is performing the act of forgiveness. However, we must let go and forgive at a deep, unconscious level, not just in a superficial manner, but also in the heart, where it really counts.

> 'It takes a lot more courage to let something go than it does to hang on to it, trying to make it better. Letting go doesn't mean ignoring a situation. Letting go means accepting what is, exactly as it is, without fear, resistance, or a struggle for control.' –Iyanla Vanzant, author and inspirational speaker.

How to let go of beliefs

Life inevitably changes us when we let go of the unalterable past.

> 'If you let go a little, you will have a little peace. If you let go a lot, you will have a lot of peace.' – Ajahn Chah, influential teacher of Buddhamma.

That is why we literally just need to get rid of our old ways of thinking, such as believing we cannot succeed. The belief that we hold creates the reality we experience, and this convinces us that our belief is true. A belief is just a thought we believe in. For example, we may believe that we cannot make money unless we work hard for it. However, there are people who make huge amounts of money by working smarter, not harder. Instead of being robotic in how we approach tasks, we must always ask ourselves if something can be done more efficiently or even eliminated altogether.

A person who believes he/she can never be rich will always be poor. That particular individual is held back by a lack of self-belief. This self-doubt creates the reality in which he/she lives. It is not the other way around: an uncontrollable reality which imposes itself on its victim.

When we realise that some of our beliefs are not the 'truth', but rather just a collection of thoughts and assumptions, we then understand they can be replaced by whatever thoughts we wish to choose.

That is why such negative thoughts of unavoidable failure must be supplanted by a set of positive beliefs, so that we can indeed fulfil our true potential. Such a change in our belief-structure does not happen overnight. Usually it takes a few months for the new positive beliefs to become truly embedded in our minds.

We always need to stay positive. There will always be setbacks. Sometimes we have to struggle. That is why it is essential that we also appreciate the success of others and to be inspired by their achievements. As well, we must exercise total control over our desires to create our new reality. Letting go of the old habitual belief that we can only strive without success is difficult. However, with our new beliefs, we will succeed in the world around us.

We mustn't give up too easily. There will still be problems, but now we can solve these much more calmly and therefore far more successfully. We can break the bad habits of drinking too much, wasting our time surfing the internet, even recover from alcohol abuse or drug addiction.

Firstly, we must acknowledge we have a problem, and then find other ways to occupy ourselves. By trusting our inner guidance, whatever it is we need to know, is revealed. That's why, we need to trust our instincts, think about what inspires us and then act appropriately. We can all find the answers we need within ourselves. It is simply a matter of living in the present, having that powerful sense of awareness, which can inform us of the truth.

All we need is the willingness to change. **We do not have to know HOW.** The universe will figure out the ways and means. Every thought we have, every word we say, is being responded to in this moment. These thoughts and words are creating our future.

There is nothing that happens by chance; everything has a meaning. Acting on pure instinct brings better results instead of thinking and deciding. Sitting back and detaching ourselves from any thoughts and emotions, allows us to accept what happens. As well, by paying attention to those moments of inspiration, those instincts that come to our mind, and simply by acting on them, our desires are fulfilled.

Truly allowing the universe to do what it needs to do is the only way forward. We picture what we want, do everything possible to acquire what we want, then hand over the rest of the process to our instincts, which will faultlessly guide us to the right place, at the right time in the right way.

The universe gives us the inspiration needed to take action. That accounts for eighty percent of the task. Many people do nothing, expecting to have it all, without making any real effort. How can the universe then respond? Would we give one of our employees a gift, if he/she just expected it and never made any effort to work for it?

Sometimes, when we think about the desire, if we pay close attention to our emotions, we might notice that we are actually frustrated by the fact that we have not yet received it. This is an expectation that the desire should have been here sooner, based on the idea that 'what we really desire, will come to us'. The frustration we feel, in effect, makes us repel what we want. We must do the opposite. Let go of any frustration, Reject such feelings. Instead, meditate. As well, although it may sound crazy, don't be afraid to cry. It's perfectly natural to do so and completely beneficial.

> 'Crying away your negative feelings releases harmful chemicals that build up in your body due to stress.' – Dr William Frey, Professor of Pharmaceutics.

The unconscious mind will somehow conceive of great ways to accomplish our desires. When it presents these great opportunities, we want to make sure our conscious mind doesn't block them with its judgement. If we keep thinking consciously about an idea or prospect our conscious mind will keep obstructing what our unconscious mind has to offer. So, the conscious mind must not impede the power of the unconscious mind and this is precisely what we mean by the phrase '*letting go*'.

How best to let the unconscious mind work as our guide

By keeping the conscious mind busy with actions, even quite trivial ones, inspired by our desires, we allow the unconscious mind to take over. This is when our unconscious mind will reveal to us great opportunities. These come to the fore when we least expect them. We then fulfil our desires fast, as quickly as possible, because we are searching for them in the right way.

Our mind guides us and so creates for us an exciting adventure. Don't be concerned as to how or when to achieve our goal; leave that to the Higher Power. All we need to know is that the direction in which we are travelling will allow us to find the right answers at the right time.

Remember!

Forgiveness is a gift we give to ourselves. Forgiving our own faults and mistakes empowers us and enables to forgive the mistakes others have made. At the same time, these acts of forgiveness to unlock the door of our own true self, where all the elements of creativity are stored.

We reward ourselves with a sense of real joy, when we unburden ourselves of all our anger and resentment, letting go of the things that weigh us down. In this way, we ensure that we can make a genuine improvement to our lives.

Enjoy living in the present moment. Bid farewell to the stress and frustration of the past. Rid ourselves of the old pessimism. Learn to fly faster and further.

We can only live in the present if we let go the past. By changing ourselves of the better, the world also changes for the better. However, letting go of what we can't change is a brave thing to do as well as being worthwhile.

Believing we can't succeed means we won't succeed. Believing in ourselves and our future success is the first essential step to success.

Our unconscious mind must become our guide. As we strive for success, the unconscious mind will reveal many wonderful opportunities for us.

15
Allowing life to flow effortlessly

What does the word 'allow' mean?

To give permission to do something,

To 'make peace' with the world around us, to accept things as they are,

To be patient, let others think what they want and not to pass judgement.

We need to identify what we want or desire and experience happiness with those things we receive or accept. This allows us to focus on our own thoughts, so that we become increasingly inspired by our ideas.

Letting things be should be one of our most important beliefs, guiding us through our lives.We must be honest and tolerant to everything and everyone. We simply have to live and allow others to be as they see fit as well. For any of us to live in a way which allows us our own personal freedom, we must make this basic principle be an essential part of our own consciousness. This, in turn, then ensures we will follow the best possible path to success. Judging others, attempting to change them or inflicting suffering on them, prevent us living our own life according to this concept. When we think about others we should do so with empathy and compassion.

That's why we should not be negative towards others or their actions. If someone is doing something that annoys us or making decisions that we know are not in one's best interest, it is reasonable to explain our objections in a calm manner. Then, we leave things be, hoping for the best on their behalf.

By accepting the rights of others to pursue their own ambitions, we must not presume we know what's best for them. Our emotions guide us. Whenever we feel pleased, we are willingly allowing others to do so as well. This is an essential aspect of life and inner growth – as well as of our success and personal fulfilment. So we must turn our thoughts and feelings to those things we want.

That means we have to take note of how we feel at this moment. In other words, we must live in the moment. This approach improves our quality of life immensely. Living in the moment or being mindful is all about living as if there is no tomorrow. To do this, we must appreciate the beauty to be found in every moment of our lives. We achieve this state of mind, when we consciously act in a way that entails real commitment, not just some vague acknowledgement; but the reward for such an effort is a richer, fuller life. If we concentrate on what is happening in the here and now, we deal with the immediate. If we don't do this, we end up worrying about things that may never even happen. In other words, we live in the moment. We don't worry about the long term. The future hasn't yet arrived. We mustn't cry over the past -- it's gone forever, never to return.

> 'When you don't flow freely with life in the present moment, it usually means that you're holding on to a past moment. It can be regret, sadness, hurt, fear, guilt, blame, anger, resentment, or sometimes even a desire for revenge. Each one of these states comes from a space of un-forgiveness, a refusal to let go and come into the present moment. Only in the present moment can you create your future.' – Louise Hay, motivational author.

Doing our best to live in the *present* and making it beautiful signifies that each moment is very important because this is where all of our feelings are, where all of our power is. This also gives us peace of mind. Nothing is more important than that we feel truly content.

There is truth in the notion, that 'if it is to be, it's up to me' i.e. our achievements are dependent on us taking the initiative, but if we don't learn the art of balancing that out with our ability to allow others their own path to happiness, we may still fail as well. It is very important that to achieve long term goals, we must keep a proper balance between our focus on what we are doing and on what we allow others to do.

Recognising that all is well in our lives – i.e. feeling prosperous, happy, and free, valued and secure, strong and energetic – means we are also allowing others to live their lives! By spending a few minutes a day feeling as if we have already acquired the things we really want, will soon bring about a complete change in our inner being. In turn, we will notice how minor miracles are suddenly happening around us. Everything will start to fall into place. Until then, we must learn as much as we can, laugh often, live for the moment and acknowledge that life is worthwhile.

Those who do get what they want find within themselves the rhythm of the universe and acknowledge that it is a part of them. In so doing, they commune with the universe, are at one with it and what they want, allowing themselves to receive their heart's desire without doubt, fear, or worry.

The concept of giving without expectation is well explained by quoting the great poet Hafiz: 'Even after all this time, the sun never says to the earth, "you owe me".' It asks nothing back. Because everything in the universe exists because of energy, allowing this elemental force into our lives is what allows us to relax and enjoy life's journey. This energy manifests itself through the process of giving, consent and serving others.

When we align ourselves with lower energy frequencies, we feel tightness somewhere in our body. It could be our stomach, neck or shoulders. We might have a headache or backache. We will feel depressed and, anxious, separate, perhaps even full of hatred most of the time. Perhaps, when we hear of all the sorrows of the world, it gets us down. Instead of watching the news, we can always choose, for example, to go for 15 minutes' walk. In so doing, we may well then feel happier and safer.

When we align ourselves with higher energy frequencies, we will feel lightness in our body and mind. There will be nearly always a feeling of fluidity and unity with everything around us: a sensation of love and warmth, hope, even excitement and passion.

One natural concept states that 'like attracts like'. So if that inner sense of rhythm within us all, which can harmonise with the natural vibration of the universe, remains low, we will attract experiences and people who will make us fail.

When we think of others and this makes us feel jealous or annoyed, then start working out why these negative thoughts invade our mind. That's why we should not take things other people say too personally. What they think and say is a reflection of them, not us. If we care too much about what other people think, in a way, we will always be their prisoner.

Knowing we can choose what we *'tune into'* is very important. Therefore, we must always keep our mind focused on the positive outcomes we are trying to achieve, rather than indulging in negative thoughts.

Remember!

Do not judge others and how they lead their lives. Instead, we have to find within ourselves that sense of fluidity which allows us to live within the moment.

By accepting that others seek their own paths, we allow ourselves to be in agreement with the spirit of our goals. Passing judgement on others, attempting to change the way they live destroys the harmony we seek within ourselves.

Our emotions guide us; because of our feelings, we can enter into that mental process, when we are fully immersed in the task at hand and the world around us seems to disappear. This is important because it allows us to live in the moment.

16
Reasons to feel contented

In our all-too-often hectic everyday lives, there always seems to be yet something else that *has to be done*! Far too easily, this modern world of targets and deadlines makes us neglect our need for some respite from the frantic pace of the daily routine, to guard those precious moments of laughter, relaxation and delight, in other words, makes us forget that we are meant to enjoy life.

Only by making a conscious effort to take time off from the otherwise incessant demands of the workplace can we truly find solace in our daily schedule. To begin with, we must simply ask ourselves how we feel. If the answer to this is in any way negative, if we are assailed by doubts or worries, then we have to focus immediately far more on the positive.

> 'When I feel good about myself, things start happening for myself. When you look up, you go up.' – Herschel Walker, retired USA professional football player.

Life cannot be serious all the time. It is also meant as much as possible to be easy and fun. Therefore, for today, let the most important thing we can think about be *the way we feel*. Our most important aim must be to seek that which we wish to be. Nothing can be more important than feeling good. This means we need to think about what pleases us the most.

When we say 'I feel good' it can mean many different things: robust health, a fine physique, limitless wealth, being at peace with oneself or in harmony with one's surroundings, to have a sense of honour, to respect and be respected, indeed, to love and be loved. Self-evidently, we like feeling good. It's wonderful. Often we are not aware of the things which prevent us from finding happiness. We have to remove the barriers between our conscious mind and our higher self-esteem, the real us, the happy us. Only by doing so can we find the goodness in life that we deserve.

Our emotions are like an internal guidance system which can ensure we are moving in the right direction. If we feel bad about ourselves, we simply go backward. However, we should remember, one way to feel good is through the act of giving, because it's aligned with our inner being. The joy we feel is a sign our thoughts are the right ones.

We create our own experiences. Feeling happy creates more positive experiences. That's why we need to engage in more lively and energetic activities. These will make us feel more positive about life. Even pamper ourselves, now and then. Find time to identify those thoughts which make us feel more at ease with ourselves. We must congratulate ourselves, whenever we succeed in a chosen task.

When we have problems

If there is a problem, don't just try to fix the problem. Far better, fix our thinking. Work out how our attitude can be improved, so that our response to any problem will be far more effective in the future. Attitude is a vital key to the door of success. Never panic! Instead, say to ourselves, 'Everything will turn out for the better.' This will reduce our feeling of unease long enough for the universe to find out a solution.

Envy, jealousy and greed

It is really important to eliminate any feelings of envy from our thoughts. Being envious is like drinking poison while waiting for the intended victim to die. We suffer from envy because we are angered by the success of others, which they achieved through their positive thinking.

Nothing is more important than that we feel good (excited, happy anticipation, full of joy and freedom, eager and optimistic) because when we have a celebration party first, then our luck turns to us, but not the other way around. Many of us seem to have forgotten how to celebrate. When we celebrate, it is an act of self-acknowledgement, demonstrating to ourselves that we have achieved another success. The act of celebration helps us stay in the present, to live in the moment. By celebrating every small step forward, our efforts gain momentum. Thomas Edison, the inventor, explained that every error we make is, nevertheless, 'a cause for celebration', because we can always learn from our mistakes. Life is a journey. That means that every step, as well as reaching a particular destination along the way, remains part of the same journey. Celebrating every success is recognition of a life well-lived.

When we fail to celebrate our successes, we are telling ourselves that we have no right to be proud of ourselves and so our self-doubt grows.

As both our moods and indeed our life improve, those who know and watch us will be wondering what this change is, and why we seem to feel so good about things. If they ask why, explain how we realised at long last that adopting a far more positive attitude is the path to success. For example, it's as if we can say to ourselves, 'At first, I felt more positive about myself and now things have begun to fall into place. I don't waste my time trying to feel good about the future. That's all wrong both in practice and in principle. That's the mistake I made for years. I thought I should wait for my luck to turn and then celebrate.'

When we feel at our best, we shall attract all the good things of heaven and earth. All the spirits of the universe will come to our help. In this way, we feel happy and appreciate as much as possible what is happening to us. This also allows us to find a greater variety of paths to true happiness. One way forward is to write down a list of things that make us feel good and go over that list daily for about 10 to 20 minutes in a relaxed way. For example, listening to songs and music can put us in a good mood, which, in turn, will help us feel as though we have already fulfilled our dreams.

Happiness

'Happiness is not in the mere possession of money; it lies in the joy of achievement, in the thrill of creative effort.' – Franklin D. Roosevelt, 32nd President of the United States.

Money can certainly make a lot of things easier and by that I mean that it helps if we have enough to be able to pay for our bills and all the necessary things in life without having to constantly worry about it.

In my opinion, living a life of meaning and purpose is the key component in anyone's quest for happiness. However, this means I would never equate money with happiness. I really don't think we need to be rich in order to be happy. Interestingly, Dr Todd B. Kashdan, scientist, public speaker and a professor of psychology at George Mason University researched that 'living a life of doing good' can give you a profound sense of meaning and purpose; cultivating a sense of curiosity can be a key ingredient to a happy and meaningful life. He also describes how the greatest opportunities for joy and personal growth happen when we enjoy the unknown and ask '*why*?' Plato, the philosopher himself, said, 'Philosophy begins in wonder.'

Therefore, the source of happiness lies within us. True happiness is a lasting feeling of pleasure and it comes when we have all of our needs satisfied. Martin Seligman, one of the leading researchers in positive psychology and author of *Authentic Happiness*, describes 'happiness as having three parts: pleasure, engagement, and meaning. Pleasure is the "feel good" part of happiness. Engagement refers to living a "good life" of work, family, friends, and hobbies. Meaning refers to using our strengths to contribute to a larger purpose.' Seligman says that all three are important, but that of the three, engagement and meaning make the most difference to living a happy life.

Sharing multiplies happiness

'Happiness cannot be travelled to, owned, earned, worn or consumed. Happiness is the spiritual experience of living every minute with love, grace, and gratitude.' – Denis Waitley, motivational speaker and writer.

Happiness involves giving freely to others and not necessarily wanting anything in return. Every person on this planet is striving to be happy. Happiness is a choice. Let ourselves be happy. Just because others don't like our preferences, doesn't mean we should worry about their opinion. We can choose to be happy by choosing to think in a positive in any moment. According to Sonja Lyubomirsky, author and one of the world's leading researchers on happiness, 'if you want to develop lifelong satisfaction, you should regularly engage in positive thinking about yourself, share your happiest events with others, and enjoy every positive experience in your life.'

Remember!

Let 'the way we feel' be the most important thing today. We will feel refreshed and be able to think more clearly.

Our least achievements are still real stepping stones towards the realisation of our greatest dreams. It is necessary that we at all times aim higher while also taking time to enjoy the achievements we've already attained. We should always celebrate our success.

Imagining success can bring about success. It is essential that we celebrate in advance an anticipated success and don't wait for our luck to turn.

Sharing multiplies happiness. It is like lighting hundreds of candles from a single flame.

Our feelings let us know we're on the right track.

Envying others' success simply leads to a greater sense of disappointment and more failure.

Instead of feeling envious, try to be inspired by the success of others.

All too often, we forget that the source of happiness lies within the centre of our spiritual being. We therefore enjoy being generous because it's aligned with our inner being.

PART FOUR

The Art of Asking Questions

17

The Importance of Asking the Right Questions

This is perhaps the most important chapter of all

Questions can be immensely powerful in their effect, changing what we think and do in our lives. They can alter our focus in an instant, transforming the way we think, so that instead of being held back by old assumptions, we can be inspired to think in new and inexhaustible ways. Questions can therefore empower us to an incredible degree.

Don't forget that whatever we focus on the most will eventually become our reality. By learning to ask ourselves empowering questions, regardless of our circumstances, we will be able to focus on new possibilities and solutions.

> 'You can tell whether a man is clever by his answers. You can tell whether a man is wise by his questions.' – Naguib Mahfouz, writer and Nobel Prize Winner.

By asking the right questions, we can discover all kinds of useful information that can help us achieve our goals. Gathering information is much like doing a jigsaw puzzle. We get pieces of information and put them together to build the bigger picture. However, our questions need to be insightful – they need to probe.

> 'It is not the answer that enlightens, but the question.' – Eugene Ionesco Decouvertes, playwright and dramatist.

Questions trigger the imagination and stimulate our creative thinking skills. They can also unconsciously focus the mind on

what we wish to achieve. They encourage us to explore and so offer many new insights.

> 'Successful people ask better questions, and as a result, they get better answers.' – Tony Robbins, author and motivational speaker.

In posing a question about our aims in life, we are not trying to find a quick answer. Instead, we are shifting the focus from one of unconscious doubt and scepticism to conscious belief in and certainty of what exists even at the present moment. On the other hand, **statements trigger our brain's logical and analytical skills and generally cause doubt and disbelief.** Statements make people judgemental.

We enjoy questions because they provide incentive, direction and focus. The right hemisphere in the brain, which is the creative and intuitive part of the mind, begins to 'open up'. As soon as a question is asked, the brain immediately begins searching for an answer. It carries on doing so, even though we might not be aware of this, until an answer can be found. For example, we can ask ourselves, 'What will I enjoy today?' or 'How can I make a positive difference in other people's lives?'

Clearly, therefore, one of the most effective ways to approach any problem is to ask questions about it. Redefining a problem in the form of a question or series of questions often clarifies far more precisely what we face and can consequently be highly effective in helping us to find a solution.

When people feel the need for change, it is generally because they are experiencing some type of disruptive influence in their lives, usually something they fear. On the other hand, their wish to alter the way things are could come from a more positive source, such as hope, aspiration, or desire. The questions we ask are the seeds of change. Questions empower us, putting us in charge of the discourse, because we are, in effect, pressurising our interlocutor to answer. As long as we keep asking questions, we are in charge of the conversation. Frequently a question cannot be immediately answered. Instead, we will mull over it for days or weeks as we work out an answer. We should not see this kind of delay as any sort of disappointment. The seed has been planted; it will soon bear fruit.

'Your mind will answer all questions if you learn to relax and wait for the answer.' – William S Burroughs, novelist and painter.

The answer will come to us when we least expect it. We simply let the universe give us the answers, allowing the universe to give us the awareness of how that can be, and see what shows up. After all, our thoughts are the results of our own inner dialogue.

That's why being able to ask the right questions is of great importance. We develop knowledge and wisdom in response to our own particular questions. Indeed, questions have always been the principal catalyst for discovery of new knowledge. If we only ask questions we already know the answers to, we don't learn or grow. In turn, clearly, therefore, we can neither explore nor innovate.

'Once you have learned how to ask the right questions you have learned how to learn and no one can keep you from learning whatever you want or need to know.' – Neil Postman, author and cultural critic.

The right question can be just the right prompt to inspire us to action, to gain better perspective, and so help us make the most of any situation. Einstein once remarked: 'If I had an hour to solve a problem and my life depended on the solution, I would spend the first 55 minutes determining the proper question to ask, for once I know the proper question; I could solve the problem in less than five minutes.' The great Greek teacher and philosopher, Socrates, taught by asking questions; he didn't give lectures or write books. His questions were formulated so as to draw out answers from his pupils. It is a form of inquiry based on discussion between individuals. This would stimulate critical thinking and lead to new ideas and fresh perspectives. Socratic questioning challenges received wisdom, while probing the supposed accuracy and completeness of conventional thinking. This process then can move people towards their ultimate goal.

Have we ever noticed that our moments of greatest enlightenment come from someone asking a powerful question? For example, by asking ourselves, **'What do I want my life to be**

like in 5 years' time?' suddenly everything seems to make a little more sense, and we begin to know what we need to do from that point forward.

Furthermore, searching questions can change aspects of our personality. **For example, by asking ourselves questions such as, 'What is the real purpose of our life? What do I absolutely love in life?'** we give ourselves a chance to challenge our own ideals. If we want to live an extraordinary life, it is vital that we know who we truly are. We each have a unique purpose in this world and to fulfil our destiny we must discover who we truly are.

Genuinely searching questions can help to create a life far higher quality. As I have already said, they drive knowledge and growth, fuelling both our creative skills and our ability to engage in critical thinking. They teach on how to focus and on what to focus, as well as therefore determining how we think and feel. Consequently, questions are powerful tools. They can ignite hope and lead to new insights but equally destroy any sense of optimism and keep us locked in a cycle of despair. That is another reason why we need to choose which questions to ask with care.

Asking a question of real value can be a great challenge. At the same time, such a high-quality question does not always demand a simple answer. Rather, it expands our range of thoughts, engages and encourages us, making us ultimately want to put our ideas into practice.

The difference in the quality of people's lives often comes down to the difference in the questions they consistently ask themselves. If we ask ourselves questions which lead nowhere, such as 'Why does this always happen to me?' or 'Why are things so unfair?' we are simply assuming no fault lies with us. Our answers will merely reinforce the assumptions behind the questions. We simply end up blaming others or some ill-defined version of fate. If we ask ourselves a question such as, 'How can we use our knowledge to help others?' we will look for answers that not only make us feel better about ourselves but also that we can do some good in this world. 'The key to achievement lies in being a "HOW" thinker, not an "IF" thinker.' (Anon.) In other words, our questions need to empower us. For example, we could ask: What could we do to make our interviews more memorable? These kinds of questions create new possibilities.

Another effective technique is to keep on asking, 'Why?' until we reach the heart of the matter. This single word can uncover our underlying beliefs and assumptions. Simply ask 'why' and then 'why' again, and again, and again like 'the annoying child', a concept coined by Derrick Jensen, author. With the word *why*, we are being forced to think deeply. It acts like a magnet that pulls us towards the truth, i.e. the knowledge we are trying to seek, enabling us to take the right steps forward. This new knowledge can make all the difference. It can change anyone's life, our own and also the lives of other people. It is an important first step making us understand how we can achieve the goals that excite us, and which will create a life we will enjoy living.

If someone asks why we do things in a certain way and the answer is, 'That's how it's always been done,' then such a response is self-evidently very de-motivating. If we don't have a proper explanation for why we're doing what we're doing, we should thank the person who asked the empowering question. We need to pay attention to those who have courage to ask why.

> 'The person who knows "how" will always have a job. The person who knows "why" will always be his boss.' – Diane Ravitch, author and historian in education.

Do we know our *why* we live our lives the way we do? In other words, what is the underlying purpose of our existence? Which beliefs are our inspirations? When we know the answer to these questions, we will find the courage to take the risks needed to forge ahead. We will stay motivated and so move our life onto an entirely new, more exciting and rewarding course. Which activities make us feel enthusiastic? Where do our natural talents and skills lie?

> 'The two most important days in your life are the day you are born and the day you find out why.' – Mark Twain, author and humourist.

By repeating our powerful requests, that is to say 'asking formed in the present tense', such as 'what do we want to accomplish? How do we define our purpose in life?' we overcome any limiting beliefs. Those are replaced with positive thoughts and beliefs. The more powerfully we ask such questions, the more it becomes internalised and our outer reality reflects our inner world. Our thoughts create our reality. (See Chapter 12.) To desire anything positive, we must only use positive words. This will bring about success, simply by saying it quietly to ourselves.

Whatever is desired, we must ask for it lovingly. We have to love ourselves first of all and then everything else falls into line. This is absolutely necessary if we are to achieve to anything in this world.

We are the person we've become today for a reason. So, we have to ask ourselves why? What has made us the person we now are? We ought to paint a mental picture of the person we once were, and see how much we've changed, and perhaps we'll discover something valuable about the person we really are today.

By asking ourselves searching questions, we are demonstrating perhaps the greatest hallmark of a highly-developed mind. Arguably, this habit is the ultimate tool for stimulating constructive habit. However, how can we therefore gain a command of this valuable mental routine? The answer, just like everything else in life, is practice, practice, practice. We have to always carry a notebook around and keep writing questions down as they occur to us. We have to question everything. At the same time, we should feel comfortable about any unanswered questions and not see them as problems, or as a necessary evil in the way of answers we seek. Instead, we should welcome them and allow ourselves to be amused by them. We will soon see the advantages in doing so.

We must ask ourselves the following questions. In this way we can then understand who we really are. As well, we can discover at the same time what is truly important to us.

For example, '*To whom or to what do I feel the most gratitude? What kind of thing would I do, if success were guaranteed? What are my greatest strengths? When was the last time I played to my strengths? What is the one thing I could willingly do for the rest of my life? Am I doing it now?*' Being able to answer these types of questions correctly allows all of us to find the real truth of our lives, but we must also remember, it is the unconscious mind which automatically finds the answers to these questions.

Consider the following variation of this kind of question and answer technique. We may well be surprised by the results.

'*What would I do if I became a mighty money magnet?*' In answer to this question, we can simply list everything that we would really love to do and buy. '*What do I absolutely love in life?*' Here, we simply have to respond by listing all our favourite activities or hobbies. Another useful list to make is of all the people we find the most inspirational. '*What are my greatest accomplishments in life so far?*' A catalogue of all our successes and the times when we have felt real excitement because of what we have achieved can have a surprisingly pleasing result. To discover which set of values we really have, we merely have to write down all those things we would do, if we weren't afraid of failure.

Self-talk

We can change the way we think for the better by the way we talk to ourselves. To use the jargon psychologists prefer, this is often called **self-talk** or **self-posed questioning**. This is an internal voice which determines how we perceive every situation. It includes our conscious thoughts as well as our unconscious assumptions or beliefs. Having a positive conversation with ourselves can be so powerful, it becomes life-changing. Negative self-talk not only adversely affects our view of ourselves but also blocks our progress. It therefore limits any chance of success and also makes us far less ambitious. Clearly, it is absolutely vital to avoid negative self-talk. For good or ill, we listen to our inner voice, just like listening to our own child when he/she needs help and, just as with a child, we need to be patient, allowing our innate voice of wisdom to flow through us.

Once we get into the habit of analysing our own self-talk, noting whether or not it's constructive, we shall find that it is much easier to inspire ourselves and others. When we change, so does the world around us.

'I just realised my lips are inside out. They should be turned inwards, because I spend most of my time talking to myself.' – Jarod Kintz, author.

Often, negative self-talk involves telling ourselves 'I can't' or 'It is too difficult'. When we say something like this, we create resistance; our brain stops working. If these kinds of thoughts occur, challenge them and ask 'Why can't I?' By asking the question in a positive way, along the lines of 'How can I (afford it etc.)?' our brain is put to work. In other words, to be successful, **we need to start saying far more, 'I can!'** One method that may be useful is merely to say 'Cancel, Cancel' each time we think or say something negative.

Therefore, we must remember to avoid asking negative questions. For example, if we ask, 'I wonder what could go wrong today,' our brain will search and search until it finds an answer and we will end up having a whole list of things that could go wrong. This then makes mishaps and mistakes all the more likely. Consequently, as we can already see, questions such as 'How did I get into this mess?' or 'Why did this happen?' lead nowhere.

On the other hand, the following types of questions do encourage success. We can easily work out which ones could help us the most:

1. How can I turn my challenges into learning opportunities?
2. How could my life be transformed if I did something I am afraid of?
3. How can I add value to other people's lives?
4. What motivates me to do my very best?
5. What do I already have that can make me into a winner?

The power of words

Words express our thoughts. Everything becomes possible by thoughts we think and words we speak; and our thoughts are made truly powerful by our emotions. This is because our words represent the inner power of the unconscious mind and have the ability to replace harmful beliefs with ones which are far more positive. For example, by saying that we love success, we stimulate the feeling of success that brings success. Love is even more powerful. When a thought is filled with love it will bring forth the thing we are thinking about in a most amazing way. This means we must only engage with the positive emotions of faith, love, enthusiasm and hope and avoid the negative emotions of fear, greed and jealousy.

'Don't be afraid of your fears. They're not there to scare you. They're there to let you know that something is worth it.' – C Joy Bell C, author.

By changing our words, we can change our brains. According to Andrew Newberg M.D., leading neuroscientist and Mark Robert Waldman, expert on communication, spirituality and the brain, 'Words can have the power to not only change how your brain controls your thoughts and emotions, but can even alter gene expression.' So we have to choose words wisely and speak them slowly. This will stop us being negative. As recent research has shown, the mere repetition of positive words like, ***compassion***, ***peace*** and ***love*** will affect specific genes and so lower our physical and emotional stress. Positive words and thoughts boost the motivational centres of the brain and enabling us to withstand and overcome far more successfully the inevitable problems we encounter in life.

According to the neuroscientists and brain communication researchers mentioned above, negative words can damage both the speaker's and listener's brain! Angry words send alarm messages through the brain that shut down the logic and reasoning centres. In fact, negative words release chemicals in our brain that cause stress. These chemicals immediately interrupt the normal functioning of our brain, impairing logic, reason, language processing, and communication. Just seeing a list of negative words for a few seconds can make a neurotic person feel worse. Indeed, they can affect all of us. The more we think about them, the more we can actually damage key structures that regulate memory and emotions, making us lose our appetite, disrupting our sleep and even our ability to experience long-term happiness. Unfortunately, our minds are hardwired to worry, a genetic feature carried over from ancestral times when there were countless threats to survival. This is because negative words and negativity in general, enlarge the amygdala – the part of the brain that processes fear and anxiety – which in turn inhibits the prefrontal cortex, the part of the brain that allows us to think and reason.

The faster we can suspend the amygdala's reaction to an imagined threat (e.g. by asking, 'Are these circumstances causing a threat to my personal survival?') the more quickly we can take action to solve the problem.

An expert on communication, spirituality and the brain, Mark Waldman, mentioned above, says working with his team of researchers, he has discovered that very few people are conscious of the way they speak. 'Inner dialogue is going on at all times in the frontal lobe (of the brain) … The left side of the brain is optimistic, focused on problem solving and decision making. But the right side is the pessimistic part of the brain, and it's constantly generating worry, fears and doubts.'

Waldman says the good news is that we can train ourselves to move to the left side of our brain through simple and quick relaxation and positivity exercises. These exercises refresh our powers of concentration and strengthen self-confidence. These, in turn, lead to an improved quality of life.

The only way to acquire this belief is through the repetition of words. Words have an extraordinary impact on both our inner and outer lives. Our habitual thoughts have a subtle but powerful influence on our state of mind. We don't realise until the chains they form are too strong be broken. However, by shifting the way we think, we can shift our entire outlook on life, for example, just by asking ourselves which is the better answer: 'I can't' or 'I don't know how yet'? We can see whether we have the right attitudes when we consider who our closest friends and acquaintances are, because they are a reflection of us. They help to create our experiences and so at least, in part, define who we are and everything else that makes and shapes us as a person. (See Chapter 22.) If people around us often say many negative things about themselves and the world in general, often repeating the downbeat and pessimistic words, this tells us a lot about the kind of people we are.

Furthermore, avoid using words like 'should' because when do, we are not accepting reality. We're talking about how we wish things were, but aren't. As Dr. Shad Helmstetter explains in his book *What to Say When You Talk to Yourself*, when we tell ourselves what we 'should' be doing, we are, without realising it, strengthening the idea that we're *not* doing it. For example, if we say, 'I should really be exercising this morning,' the unspoken ending to that sentence is, '…but I'm not.' We have to replace the word 'should' with something far more positive and active. For example, instead of saying, 'I should do more yoga,' remind ourselves of why we want to do some yoga: 'I feel great when I do yoga a few times each week.'

In truth, there is no mystery, no amazing, magic formula to self-improvement. **Simply by asking the right questions, using the best possible words and avoiding negative expressions,** we can make real and lasting changes to our lives.

Practical Steps:

One of the best ways forward is to state desires and goals as **interrogative sentences**. For example, 'How else can I improve my performance at work? What is the next step forwards? Who can give me the best advice?'

Another useful method is for us to stand in front of a mirror and look at ourselves. Then we have to look at our posture. We need to stand tall and to be able to look ourselves in the eye. Then we can begin to feel confident as we repeat our desires in the form of inspiring questions. For example, 'How can I increase my wealth? What motivates me to do my very best?' With these particular words, this exercise makes us focus on creating wealth and removes any doubts. We will soon notice improvements after a while. We can, of course, use the same technique with different words when wishing to improve our life in any other way. To empower ourselves even further, we can add, 'I choose to create what I love to create and I am so grateful for it.'

A different technique is to relax by sitting comfortably, empty the mind of all thoughts and worries and take couple of deep breaths. Our brain waves will slow down until we enter the theta state of mind. It is essential to say out loud each of our desires in a slow and confident tone as if we believe that our dreams have already become reality.

Mentoring

As John C. Crosby – the Executive Director of the Greater Philadelphia Chapter of the Uncommon Individual Foundation – puts it, 'Mentoring is a brain to pick, an ear to listen, and a push in the right direction.'

Even the most brilliant of us all can only succeed by learning from others. Sir Isaac Newton generally regarded as the greatest mathematics, as well as being the father of modern physics, admitted the debt he owed others, when he said, 'If I have seen further, it is by standing on the shoulders of giants.'

This is also why Charlie "Tremendous" Jones – author and motivational speaker, tells us, 'You will be the same person in five years as you are today except for the people you meet and the books you read.'

Mark Zuckerberg learnt so much from Steve Jobs, Bill Gates from Warren Buffet and, indeed, Richard Branson was greatly influenced by the advice he received from the late British airline entrepreneur, Sir Freddie Laker.

The easiest way to become an expert at something is to find a mentor. We must of course always seek guidance from those who have been successful. In order to search for those genuine leaders and find the one whom we need as a mentor, we have to choose carefully, do our homework and avoid the charlatan. Once, we have found the right person make the right approach to him/her and ask the obvious questions, such as, 'How did you do what you accomplished?' Once we have received the best advice possible, we too can be successful.

We should never forget our imaginary friends! In other words we can seek help and guidance from those who have already passed away. We do this by reading everything written about them and then follow their teachings. It helps us all to imagine what course of action or advice that person would give us if he/she knew us personally. Doing this always allows us to find a new perspective, when confronted by seemingly insoluble problems and also enables us to think of new ideas and to become inspired once more. In addition, through positive self-talk with our imaginary friends we increase our self-esteem.

Remember!

The right kinds of questions can generate a great deal of information, which can then change our focus in an instant, transforming our state of mind from the limiting to the empowering.

Asking a question is more empowering than merely making a statement. This is because it triggers the imagination, expands our knowledge and stimulates creative thinking skills.

The brain loves questions. This is because questions encourage us to look for answers and in this way provides incentive, direction and focus.

Quality questions create a quality life and have the power to engage us and to shift our state of mind.

Our mind will answer all questions if we learn to relax and wait for the answer. This can often happen in an instant, when we least expect it.

We need to affirm our goals and desires in the form of interrogative sentences, commencing with the words **why** or **how**. This approach can have a really powerful effect and makes a real and lasting change to our day to day living.

Why is the most powerful word with which to form a question. When we work out **why**, we will find the courage and natural talents to take the risks needed for success.

Repetition of our most heartfelt desires overcomes any doubts. They are replaced then with positive thinking and real personal belief.

Some people find it best to state their goals in the present tense, starting their declarations with words such as, 'I am… I have… I feel great to be…' and so forth. In so doing, we are already thinking as if our stated goal is already a reality.

Highly-developed minds always question why. Just like everything else in life, with practice anybody can improve his/her way of thinking.

We must monitor our *self-talk*; always keep it positive note. Positive self-talk can make us feel good about ourselves and the things we do in our lives. It is like hearing an optimistic voice in your head.

Optimistic words and phrases stimulate the motivational centres of the brain and help us build to face life's inevitable problems with greater success.

PART FIVE

'I did then what I knew how to do. Now that I know better, I do better.' – Maya Angelou, author, poet, actress, and singer.

18
Goal Setting

Clearly defined goals give us all a long-term vision as well as short-term motivation. We must decide what we want for the future: money, skills, etc. Hopefully by now you have made a list. If not, then start making one now, including anything which is both motivating and inspiring.

The next step is to stay motivated, remembering all those powerful reasons, which made us set particular goals in the first place.

> 'People often say that motivation doesn't last. Well, neither does bathing, that's why we recommend it daily.' – Zig Ziglar, author and motivational speaker.

It may sound paradoxical, but it's true that the fastest way is not always the right way, but the right way will always end up being the fastest way! Ironically, those who make a long-term commitment to their goals are the ones who will not take as long to get results, as those who look all the time for shortcuts. So for any desires, always look for the right things to do. This must be a lifetime goal. Those small steps in the right direction help us reach our goals far faster than any elusive shortcuts. Searching for those shortcuts, which only turn out to be dead-ends, can waste a lifetime. On the other hand, it's never too late to do the right thing.

That's why, when we hear successful people talking, they give the impression that they know exactly where they want to go. Everything revolves around *how to get there*. **They know their destination. All they consider is which ways are best for them to achieve their aims.** By learning from their example, after a while our ability to do the right thing will be greatly enhanced.

By establishing a particular goal, the way forward will also appear.

In other words, how we achieve something is nothing to worry about. Instead, all we have to do is follow our intuition.

Setting our goals has a touch of magic about it, as it is **the first step** to realising our dreams. It is vital that we write them down in the present tense. A goal that has not been written down has no value. It only becomes real when it has been written down. Writing has this power to make the goal real, because it forces us to clarify what we want, motivates us and provides a filter for other opportunities. A research study conducted by Dr David Kohl, Professor Emeritus at Virginia Tech, has discovered that 80% of Americans say they don't have any specific goals. People who regularly write down their goals earn nine times as much over their lifetime as people who don't.

By setting goals that are clear and realistic, we have a clear target of where we want to be. When we work towards that goal, we improve in terms of self-confidence and self-esteem, and end up believing far more in our own abilities.

'Goal-setting illuminates the road to success just as runway lights illuminate the landing field for an incoming aircraft.' – Nido Qubein, businessman and motivational speaker.

Every time we dream of a new goal, we plant a little seed in the universe. Focusing on, thinking about and expecting that goal to come true are all the same as watering that seed. Look at that list on a daily basis. Read it out loud. Let it become a mantra and even an act of meditation.

As we apply more thought to the goal, shoots finally begin to sprout and push out of the ground. But, too often, it's at this point that we suddenly change our mind. When we do that, we simply chop down those very same shoots. No beautiful plant will grow. All we have done is wasted our time and effort and gone back to the beginning.

The second step is thinking big; dreaming even unrealistic, incredible dreams. This is because when we do so we really stretch ourselves.

That's why we mustn't be afraid to take giant leaps. We can't cross a chasm in two small steps. We must widen our goals. Remember, for any of us, anything is possible, so long as we desire it strongly enough, believe in it, and take those steps **inspired by our desires** towards our chosen goals. After all, if we had a genie ready to grant our wishes, would we ask for something trivial, like a bar of chocolate?

So, aim higher, dare to dream big and reach further.

'Dare to dream! If you did not have the capability to make your wildest wishes come true, your mind would not have the capacity to conjure such ideas in the first place. There is no limitation on what you can potentially achieve, except for the limitation you choose to impose on your own imagination. What you believe to be possible will always come to pass – to the extent that you deem it possible. It really is as simple as that.' – Anthon St. Maarten, international psychic medium.

The bigger the goals, the more excited about them we can be. If we don't feel a little nervous when setting our goals, the odds are we're thinking too small. So we need to apply this principle. Do our goals excite us? Do they scare us a little? Those that do are probably the right ones. We must allow ourselves to grow by exposing our vulnerabilities and insecurity. We should not simply live inside our comfort zone. If we simply play safe, we go nowhere.

Our goals have to be measurable, but inspirational enough to fill every part of our vision. We have to be specific about exactly what we want. This means we must take our time, know all the ins and outs, the colours, size and quality of what we need and paint the picture in our mind, but avoid setting any strict deadlines for our desires to come true. This is because if we do so, we only become tenser. We start to assume that things should be happening sooner than when we are ready for them. If we stick to a goal we will reach it. Sometimes we may push too hard when we just need to let go and take the pressure off. Reading a book (like this) or watching a motivational movie and expecting the best may help to get us realigned with our Creator. To expect is to believe and to know the magic of believing. Therefore, our expectations have a positive impact on us, as we seek to achieve our goals.

'Life is largely a matter of expectations.' – Horace, Quintus Horatius Flaccus, known in the English-speaking world as

Horace, leading Roman lyric poet during the time of Augustus.

When we expect the best, we release a magnetic force in our mind which attracts the best to us.

When we expect the worst, our mind repulses the best from us. If we change our habits by learning to expect positive results, it makes everything possible. Our expectations cause our energy to flow out into the world and affect other energy systems.

Hybrid goal setting

This concept promotes the idea that one can set long term general goals – maybe three at the most – which are punctuated by short term, unplanned, but inspired deeds.

It is like a long drive at night, when we already know the destination, but the car headlights only show a small part of the journey at a time. We go as far as we can see and when we get there, we are able to see further.

A rather different approach

'You don't always need a plan. Sometimes you just need to breathe, trust, let go and see what happens.' – Mandy Hale, author.

We have some limited choice (setting our life's purpose), but not total choice – because if we have total choice, we would be doing exactly what we want to do, and we would make a mess of it.

Going through life without a **'detailed plan'** is easy, because in a plan there is always an element of fear. After all, we always worry that it might go wrong. On the other hand even if we don't trust the universe, it is always taking care of us.

Nevertheless, being afraid of planning things is wrong. We don't have to plan everything in detail. This means, if we prefer not to do so, we don't have to set goals, but just get connected to the consciousness of the universe, which will guide us faultlessly.

Finally, we should expect good things to happen. Then we'll notice a series of beautiful coincidences pushing us in the direction we want. We must not ignore these coincidences as they are our path to freedom, and may well be given to us by the universe.

Remember!

To achieve our lifetime goals we must take those small steps in the right direction and avoid the trap of shortcuts, which always turn out to be dead ends.

Pay attention to the conversations of successful people. They explain that they know exactly where they want to go. They only questions they have are about how to reach their goals.

When we dream of a new goal, we plant a little seed in the universe. Focusing on, thinking about and expecting this goal are all the same as watering that seed.

Once we have implanted in our deeper mind the idea of what we wish to attract, we must not be preoccupied by the notions of how we are going to achieve our goals.

We should never forget that focusing on the **_how_** will only close off the unlimited number of potential alternatives of which we are not yet aware.

A strict deadline makes things tense. To relax, read a book, breathe deeply or watch a motivational movie.

A plan is like a set of instructions to execute our goal. While implementing a strict plan there is always an element of fear. For this reason, a plan may not be the right thing. Sometimes we just need to breathe, trust, let go and see what happens.

Write down all our goals in the present tense and visualise them every morning and every night.

19
Making our desires come true

How can we make our dreams come true? We need to create the right conditions. Therefore we must understand that we create our new reality through our emotions. When we say to ourselves something like, 'I feel good,' these kinds of emotions will create the conditions which in turn allow the universe to work effortlessly on our behalf. That is to say, by controlling our thoughts though positive feelings, we will rapidly attract success.

To start with, we have to take a good look at our life right now. Where do we live? What kind of car do we drive? How much money is in the bank? What is missing in our life? Once more, it is highly recommended to look in the mirror. What do we see? Whatever we see, it will be, in one way one another, the truth.

'I am a big believer in the 'mirror test'. All that matters is if you can look in the mirror and honestly tell the person you see there, that you've done your best.' – John McKay, film director.

We are responsible for everything in our life so accept responsibility for where we are today or we'll be powerless to change those things we want to change. Most people don't take personal responsibility for the way they live. They honestly believe the cause of their present circumstances lies beyond their control. Just be aware we are the ones who attracted every person, every job, every idea, every joy and every bit of pain into our life.

If we don't pursue what we want, we will never have it. **In other words, if we don't ask, the answer will always be no.** We must always go forward. Otherwise, we'll always be stuck in the same place.

'We cannot become what we need to be by remaining what we are.'
– Oprah Gail Winfrey (media proprietor, actress and producer.)

This, in turn, means that it is always better to leave behind pains, sorrows, to forget about any grudges or fears, as well as to replace hesitant words like *wish*, *try* and *should* with a confident assertion, such as *I will*. To experience real luck, we need to work smarter, be more proactive, most importantly, work out '**why**' we do what we do. This might mean sometimes that to achieve our goals, we have sometimes to make waves. For example, we mustn't be discouraged by setbacks. Instead, we have to be daring, be open to new ideas and remain flexible until our goals are achieved. In brief, making waves means to be boldly unconventional and to have the courage to do something.

Have my thoughts created all this?

Whatever we see in the physical universe has been created in one way or another by our thoughts. This is because they are the creative force which then takes a physical form. The more creative our thoughts are, the more powerful our ability to create becomes. Everything starts as a thought. That's why it is crucial to pay attention to each of them. They influence our feelings and these consequently control our actions. By controlling our thoughts, we can create our chosen reality. Any failure to have a proper command of our thoughts will result in our life becoming seemingly a series of random events, leaving us at the mercy of circumstances beyond our control.

For example, if we worry about getting all those bills paid, all we will do is create more panic. Our thoughts are nothing more than frequencies or vibrations that resonate with similar vibrations which already exist. To explain this more clearly, place two guitars side by side and pluck a string on one of them. The string on the other guitar will start vibrating, even though we haven't touched it. It is the principle of resonance. Fascinating, isn't it?

That is why we can say, that our consciousness is like a radio station. We can emit signals and receive them. Sometimes we may receive signals from others, sometimes we send them instead. Knowing when to send and when to receive is one of the most important lessons we must learn if we are to be successful in life. It is a question of knowing when to create and when to experience. We cannot constantly create, for we would miss out on so much knowledge that others can offer us. On the other hand, if we only experience things, we will never create anything of our own.

In every moment, we have a choice about what we want to do, and what we want to decide. If we don't exercise this power nothing happens in our life, at least not what we want.

'It is our choices that show what we truly are, far more than our abilities.' – J. K Rowling, novelist.

Manifesting our dreams

'If you're already pursuing your dream, pat yourself on the back. You're doing awesome.'

'The distance between your dreams and reality is called action.' – Anon.

When we dream, we create a reality in which events happen around us, and in which we perceive other people as individuals separate from ourselves. In this dream, everything seems very real. But when we wake, we realise that everything in the dream was actually a creation of our own unconscious mind.

'The same process of reality-generation occurs in waking consciousness. The difference is that now the reality that is created is based on sensory data, and bears a closer relationship to what is taking place in the real world. Nevertheless, however real it may seem, it is not actually the real world. It is still an image of that world created in the mind like a dream. It seems undeniable that out there, around you, independent and apart from you, exists as a physical world, utterly real, solid and tangible. But the world of your experience is no more out there than are your dreams.' – Thomas Herold, author.

Defeats are only temporary. On the other hand, if we give up, then setbacks do become permanent. Therefore, do not be afraid of failure. Only those who dare to fail, achieve great success.

> 'Life is not waiting for the storm to pass; it's about learning to dance in the rain.' – Vivian Greene, novelist.

> 'Dream lofty dreams, aim higher, reach farther, dream bigger and as you dream, so shall you become.' – Anon.

How big are our dreams? For our dreams to inspire us, they must take us out of our comfort zone.

Always retain a strong vision of what we want. Use it as a guide as we strive for success. A very powerful aid in this regard, is to write out in detail, what our dream is. This process as well will trigger our unconscious into action.

Remember, however:

> 'Vision without execution is hallucination.' – Thomas Edison, an inventor and businessman.

We must keep our eyes and mind open for clues in the universe that will tell us through our feelings if we are on the right path, or if we might need to alter our vision to a lesser or greater degree.

At the same time, have we ever wondered why some people seem to walk around with a dark cloud hovering over them and others appear to bring their own sunshine wherever they go? The former are generally unhappy, willingly finding things to complain about and, of course, nothing seems to go their way, whereas the latter walk on the same earth, feeling gratitude for the lives they live, have a positive outlook, and easily create the lives they want. In both cases, these individuals are very much creating their own destiny based on the universal truth that **like attracts like**. If we focus on the positive, we will get positive results. If we focus on the negative, everything fails.

Of course, we can't just say, 'I want £100, 000,' and focus all of our attention on that desire and that's what we get. There's more to it than that – actual hard work, for one thing! But, there is a spiritual element to all of this as well. Sometimes the universe has other plans for us, or perhaps we aren't ready to make them happen just yet.

There needs to be a strong connection with what we want and what we're destined for. We might have realised that there is some reason why things haven't happened exactly how we wanted them to. Don't let this stop us from trying, though. If we never try to hit the target once, then we can guarantee there will be a one hundred percent failure rate. We have to have faith in our instincts, which will become stronger the more we become self-aware. Self-awareness can be improved through meditation. Asking ourselves a series of searching questions, analysing our answers can also help bring more insight.

At the same time, we have to really believe in ourselves and our vision. If we really want to do something, we'll find a way. If we don't, we'll find an excuse. It must always be a question of **when we can**, **NOT** *if* we can. Self-doubt always has a negative effect, which will prevent our **dreams** from coming true. So, we must be aware of any such doubts and always understand that hesitating in this way can be overcome, when we realise that both fears and desires exist only in the mind. The more we accept our fears, the more we will make them come true instead of our dreams.

Dreams don't necessarily come true but they do take us in the right direction. That's why we must travel in the same direction as our dreams.

We don't have to know the exact end point but only the direction in which we must go. Neither do we have to know exactly how we are going to get there; the **'how'** will become apparent all in good time. That's another reason why we need to take one step at a time.

'I move forward in my life every day, even if it's only a tiny step, because I know that great things are accomplished with tiny moves, but nothing is accomplished by standing still.' – Zig Ziglar, author, and motivational speaker.

Live in the moment, while holding onto our dreams and allow them to unfold as they are meant to. This means we should never think about the future or the past. We should only ever live in the present. This allows the mind to be focused on where we are, so that all our creative energy leads to the realisation of our goal. If we are totally focused on what we want for our future, then we are focused on the new, striving towards that which we still don't possess but want. Feeling confident that things will play out as they are supposed to while we gently guide them along is a necessary part of the path to success. We will then also find that there is perfection in everything that happens along the way.

We can, therefore, describe life as a journey, an adventure, we must all undertake. When we take those first uncertain steps to a new destination, to a new and greater dream, this same dream will draw us towards those acts of creation and achievement, we are destined for. They are the sheer joys of life, the real reason for getting out of bed every morning. Let's enjoy the journey! Let's remember to celebrate all of our successes along the way.

Clearly, everything is up to us. If it is to be, it's up to ME. We can do it. Let's believe in our dreams. We only harm ourselves if we think that the whole of our life is predetermined and we have no control over it, instead of thinking of ourselves as someone who can achieve greatness. Understanding that we have the power to do amazing things means we can make them happen. Waiting for fate to manifest itself is like believing God has given us the gift of sight but we then expect Him to do the seeing for us.

Things occur because of our state of being, not the other way around. Being happy creates the happiness in which we can live. It is what we feel inside that makes us what we are. Having the right feelings, can create the dreams we wish to fulfil. We have to decide **right now** what those feelings should be, so that our future prospects are secured. This means we must trust our inner voice. At all costs, we need to avoid being paralysed by indecision. That is even worse than making the wrong decision. That's why we have to live in the present, remember the past, and not fear the future, for it doesn't exist and never shall. There is only the now.

'The best time to plant a tree was 20 years ago. The second best time is now.' (Chinese Proverb)

Remember!

By feeling happy and optimistic we can make our dreams come true. Our thoughts and feelings are the way to make our dreams a reality.

Ask ourselves **why** we do what we do. Then circumstances will begin to favour us more and more.

Every choice we make is a seed that we sow, which we must harvest at some time in our lives. Be careful how we choose, for our choices tell the world the kind of person we really are.

Keep pursuing our dreams, aim higher and higher. Don't stay in our comfort zone. Motivate ourselves. Find inspiration and take action.

Having a vision is a great start; it lets us see where we're going. It is a source of hope, courage and perseverance in the midst of difficulty.

It is important to develop a plan around a clearly defined vision.

Remember to celebrate all of our successes along the way. When we don't, we are telling ourselves that we haven't done enough to be proud of. This makes us suffer to a greater degree from self-doubt.

What we focus on determines our reality. All possibilities exist in the universe but we have to define the reality we want to experience.

20
Accumulating Wealth

A great desire for wealth brings wealth. Our desires are answered according to the universal law of action and reaction or cause and effect. The thought is the action and the reaction is the response from the creative mind.

Our ideas and thoughts are like seeds; allow them to lie in the soil. Therefore, we must be patient and let time pass. One day, we will reap our reward, so long as we protect our seed bed from past resentment and bitterness. Nourishing the soil with faith and expectation, is just like letting a planted seed grow. We mustn't interfere in this process. Instead, we simply wait.

In our real garden, we can easily trust nature and all its gifts provided by the same Creator. In the same way we can have a great harvest, by investing in ourselves, letting the seeds of our desires grow at their own pace. At the same time, we have to remember, the best investment we can make is in **ourselves**, so as to make the most of our talents. The Creator knows that we are interested. Through His power, we will find inspiration.

When it comes to success we have to pay the full price in advance. So, we must make the necessary commitment, accepting however long it takes to start to make progress, which is why we can't give up or falter.

'To become a champion, fight one more round.' – James Corbett, independent journalist.

If we begin to doubt, bear in mind, success could just be around the corner. That's why we have to always have a positive mental attitude.

'I demolish my bridges behind me… then there is no choice but to move forward' – Fridtjof Nansen, scientist and Nobel Peace Prize laureate.

If time is tough we must get tough, or as Knute Rockne a football coach puts it, 'When the going gets tough, the tough get going'. This sort of attitude wins the greatest victories.

Remember that 99% of success is created in the mind.

We are entitled to believe we were born to win, born to be rich; deserve to be wealthy simply because we were born on this planet. Successful individuals take the time to plan and set the right priorities. They evaluate their efforts, check if they exemplify their values and strive for mutually beneficial solutions. They take the concept and consider as much as possible any legal, financial, and sales and marketing ramifications. They research, calculate how valid their plans are, and then they give their time and risk their money when executing their plans. Success is the progressive realisation of a worthy ideal. We become what we think about; all of us are self-made but only a few of us ever admit it.

Success is the result of good judgement, and that, in turn, is the result of experience, but experience often comes about because of the mistakes we make.

'Learn from the mistakes of others. You can't live long enough to make them all yourself.' – Eleanor Roosevelt, politician, First Lady of the U. S.

'When you find your path, you must not be afraid. You need to have sufficient courage to make mistakes. Disappointment, defeat, and despair are the tools God uses to show us the way.' – Paulo Coelho, novelist.

Success is never about our resources, but rather it's about our resourcefulness. Many people believe that they need to have a sizable chunk of money, the right connections or a college degree in order to be considered truly 'successful' in life. Rather than let a lack of resources stop us, we must see this as a challenge to be resourceful!

'Empty pockets never held anyone back. Only empty heads and empty hearts can do that.' – Norman Vincent Peale, author and a pioneer of 'positive thinking'.

All successful people have high self-esteem; they like themselves. The more we like ourselves, the more we like other people and in return they like us. Without being arrogant, this feeling of being happy with ourselves is an essential element for any personal success. However, our most valuable financial asset is our earning ability. To double our income, we double our earning ability. We do this through *leveraging – the ability to do more with less.* The concept of *leverage* applies to both money and people. For example: the most junior employees earn the least although within a company, they will do most of the work, whereas middle management, who are far fewer in number, individually earn far more. This is because they have the power of leverage over the lower rank employees. This works all the way up the company structure. Therefore, the Managing Director receives the highest salary because he/she can leverage everyone else.

However, we should never forget, no matter how hard we try, how well we work, while attempting to climb the corporate ladder; it can easily be the case that someone else will hold you back unfairly.

So a better way to achieve leverage for ourselves is to look outside our job. We can work out how to build a business or to get a better return on our money by investing it in real estate or on the stock market.

'If you really want to dramatically increase your income, then you need to increase your leverage. This is not an overnight process, as you need to learn more skills and take action to achieve the results you want. However, the sooner you start… the sooner you see results. Ten years from now, you may have gotten a few salary increases, but I can guarantee you won't have doubled your income through your job. However, in ten years you could use your spare time to build a business and investment portfolio that doubles your income.' – Craig Dewe, blogger.

To be more financially successful one needs a clear understanding of the concepts such as having a positive attitude, self-confidence and the role of capital.

Being rich and successful does not begin from being born into a wealthy family, or by being naturally 'lucky', nor does it come from working so hard that we never have any spare time. Taking full responsibility (meaning 'the ability to respond') for what happens in our life is a sure way to succeed. If we accept responsibility, we are in a position to do something about it.

> 'When we take responsibility, we are telling ourselves and the universe, "I am able to respond to what's happening in my life, and I am not a victim." The unsuccessful people are not taking 100% responsibility for their lives and they blame others, the government, the economy, the weather etc.' – Noah St. John, author.

> 'Having a victim mentality, blaming external circumstances for your problems, believing it's not within your power to change, is the surest way to avoid improving your life. To change what's wrong in your life, you must believe you're the one in control. Don't blame, complain, or criticize. Accept full responsibility for everything in your life, whether you caused it or not; even external problems can have internal solutions.' – Tom Murcko, blogger.

If finding someone or something to blame becomes more important than finding ways to put things right, then we have a big problem. It may give us the false belief that we have found a solution, but, in reality, we've done nothing of the sort and are no nearer to understanding the causes of what has gone wrong.

We need to be big enough to accept when we have made a mistake. By admitting it to ourselves and to any other interested party, we can then find ways, if possible, to make things better. If something doesn't work out, we should try to be more creative and think of an entirely new approach or even head in a different direction. Learning to relax while we still do not actually know why something failed to work out will allow us to gain a better perspective on things.

Attitude

A positive attitude makes all the difference. Without it there can only be failure. A positive attitude takes us in a right direction and is like a blueprint for future success. Having a positive attitude will always create new and exciting possibilities, whereas being negative simply destroys any future prospects. More than anything, we have to believe in what we want. We can often change our circumstances by changing our attitudes for the better. If we don't like something, change it. If we can't change it, change our attitude.

Of course, sometimes we cannot change our circumstances – at least in the short term. For example, we may feel trapped by the job we already have but we can't simply quit because we still have to pay the bills. To solve this type of problem, it is necessary to change our perceptions. This means giving ourselves a new focus: something which will inspire us, such as retraining, attending motivational courses, or even laying the ground work for an independent business. There is never any need to despair.

Self-confidence

Self-confidence is a key ingredient; we succeed in direct proportion to our level of confidence. We must be confident that we can do whatever it takes to make our dream become true. When we change our state of mind for the better, our environment automatically changes. In other words, believe to achieve. When we learn to live without worrying about the opinion of others, we live our dream – because we can make it happen. Dreams do come true for those who dare to believe in themselves. It is never too late to begin living our own dream. We must start right now by believing in ourselves.

Capital

Capital, metaphorically speaking, is a force that raises the productivity and creates wealth. It refers to financial resources available to start a business. Therefore, it is the life blood of a business and consists of our own contributions, somebody else's share, as well as our mental, emotional and physical strength. There are countless examples of many successful businesses starting with scarce resources. That's why many successful businesses are founded with little or no financial capital but their owners all have the right attitude. In this regard, for example, one possibility is to look into a very low cost networking also known as MLM (multi-level marketing) franchise business with a well-established organisation where its representatives generate substantial monthly incomes.

How to accumulate wealth

We should think of wealth as being something fluid, not static. We have to continually act and react, in spite of any discomfort, discouragement, uncertainty, fear and failure. Nothing ever stays still. Everything always needs to keep on changing, growing and being reborn: money, people, and relationships. If we block this *flow*, then we can't become or remain prosperous.

> 'Develop success from failures. Discouragement and failure are two of the surest stepping stones to success.' – Dale Carnegie, writer, who has also developed well-known courses in self-improvement.

As a general rule, those who become very wealthy run their own business. However, we do not teach the young how to be entrepreneurs (an employer) in the real world – in schools, colleges and universities. Schools focus on academic and professional skills, but not on financial skills. This even applies to those who have great artistic skills. There is nothing romantic in a superb painter living a life of poverty. Therefore, our children today need a more sophisticated education, for the current system is not delivering the goods. (See Chapter 23.)

To be successful in business, we must always have a winning attitude, allied to a clear goal, a thought-through plan and willingness to put everything into action. In this way we develop our skills, while doing what we enjoy. At the same time, all this can lead to a great commercial success.

We need to find a business that expresses our true purpose or passion in life. By so doing, we start to live according to the true purpose of our life.

1. A Clear Goal

Our goal must be clear, precise and above all **what we would love to achieve.**

> 'You can only become truly accomplished at something you love. Don't make money your goal. Instead, pursue the things you love doing, and then do them so well that people can't take their eyes off you.' – Maya Angelou, author, poet, and actress.

If we can't see the target, we can't hit it; if we can see the target, then keep on shooting until we do hit it.

This also means we are taking charge of our own lives by beginning something we have always wanted to do. If the goal seems overwhelming, we must start on a small scale. Small steps can eventually lead to big changes. However, to reach these demanding goals, from the very beginning always think and behave like a winner.

We can really achieve what we want, create what we want to create and so choose who we want to be. We simply have to make the right choices. The most crucial part in all of this is to DECIDE to make our wishes to become facts. It doesn't matter if we think all of this is beyond our control.

> 'If everything seems under control you are not going fast enough,' – Mario Andretti, world champion racing driver.

Nor does it matter if we can't yet see how we'll get from A to B. Most of those resources will come to us naturally AFTER we have made the decision to go ahead, but not before. (See Chapter 18) All we have to do believe in our dream.

'All men who have achieved great things have been great dreamers.' – Orison Swett Marden, inspirational author.

2. Well-thought Plans

'Without leaps of imagination or dreaming, we lose the excitement of possibilities. Dreaming, after all, is a form of planning.' – Gloria Steinem, a journalist.

We need to work out all the details of what can we do, considering all our present abilities and resources. We must understand what is necessary for us to do to achieve our goal. This means making a list, setting priorities and carrying out each week's tasks based on importance rather than according to deadlines. This makes us consistent and allows us to make sure we accomplish a small part of our big goal every day.

'Do the difficult things while they are easy and do the great things while they are small. A journey of a thousand miles must begin with a single step.' – Lao Tzu, philosopher and poet.

We must sharpen our mental skills through regular physical activity, meditation, yoga, prayers and wider reading.

A goal without a plan is a fantasy. Every plane has a flight plan. A mistake in any calculation, even of just one degree, will make the plane fly thousands of miles off course. The same happens with our lives. We must find our flight plan and stick to it, not allow ourselves to deviate from our chosen course.

'There are no short cuts to any place worth going.' – Beverly Sills, operatic soprano.

3. Will to Act

'Don't wait around for your life to happen to you. Find something that makes you happy and do it. Everything else is just background noise.' – George Mason, statesman.

Simply working hard will get us nowhere. Even working smart will achieve little. It's not about work. Of course we still have to do some work but we don't have to force anything. We need to do things in the correct way, the inspired way. This means our work becomes fun and the quality of our performance is elevated. To be inspired, we can go for a walk, a run, or visit the gym. There are two great advantages of exercise: first, it's healthy for our body. Second, it forces us to spend time thinking. As well, we can read inspiring books, perform acts of kindness, listen to uplifting music or watch an inspiring video. Whatever we choose, inspiration is absolutely within our reach, anytime we seek it.

There is no substitute for inspired action. Twenty per cent of this action should be put into building the business and 80% into thinking, learning and training. We should not worry if sometimes we're unsure of what action we need to take. In these circumstances, is best to begin at once to channel our thoughts towards what we're trying to attract. The answer we seek and the action we need will come to us.

Napoleon Hill stated, 'take a few steps, small steps commonly known as "baby-steps" – towards your goal.' As we take action, events and coincidences will guide us towards the end result.

'Do what you can, with what you have, where you are.' – Theodore Roosevelt statesman, author, and the 26th President of the U.S.

So as long as we start off by laying the best possible foundations, we can make progress. We should go with the flow, (see Chapter 15) follow our intuition and be inspired. All this will lead us to new and exciting opportunities and people. **We turn these opportunities into good luck through our own inspired actions.** The rest will take on a life of its own and we will find the best way forward. Working in this way, which complements our true nature and passions, will allow us to achieve anything.

One of the cardinal sins in life is to over-analyse. We should not worry too much about whether we are doing the right thing. We need to live our lives and act on our beliefs in the way we think to be right. Clarity may come to us as an inspired thought. It may be an idea that springs up while reading a book or something a friend tells us – the possibilities are endless! The way this happens, is not important. All we need do is trust that the answer will come.

Edison, the famous inventor, was known to have said, 'Ideas come from space. This may seem impossible and hard to believe but it's true. Ideas come from out of space.' Edison was referring to intuition. He claimed that's how most of his ideas came to him. That's why we ought to listen to the quiet promptings of the heart. In the still, inner peace of the mind, we can hear our intuition.

'When you become quiet, it just dawns on you.' – Thomas Edison.

Trying too hard to find a solution simply means we drive away any chance of success.

Here are some ideas that may help us to rid our negative beliefs about money

If we are programmed to struggle and always spend more than we earn somehow, it's because of our mind-set as regards money. On a positive note, this is something we can change. The bad news is these hidden beliefs which hold us back have been programmed into our mind, although we never realised it. Changing them takes time.

We must ask ourselves what we *think* about money. Literally, how do we *feel* about it? What are our spending and saving habits? Are we focused on saving a little extra? Do we learn new money habits from reading what the experts tell us? Making some money is easy, but to become rich requires real skill.

When we are struggling financially it is a big challenge to feel rich or wealthy. Nevertheless, it helps if we can make ourselves imagine what it is like to feel wealthy even though we don't have enough money. To begin with, we need to focus on things we should feel grateful for in our life. Saying just two words of gratitude to the Creator – 'thank you' – for all the positives in our lives will suffice. We'll soon then find more and more things that we can feel grateful for, and quickly enough things will begin to pick up for us. This will include making more money.

'I always knew I was going to be rich. I don't think I ever doubted it for a minute.' – Warren Buffett, business magnate, and philanthropist.

We mustn't be upset by any problems, but instead there is always a need to keep on learning. At the same time, it is a terrible mistake to act out of spite or fear.

'Don't let the fear of losing be greater than the excitement of winning.' – Robert Kiyosaki, self-help author, motivational speaker.

Positive attitudes will attract more money to us, especially when we treat money as a beloved friend and hold no negative beliefs about it – e.g. that it is evil or filthy etc. As well, the unconscious responds very well to an exact amount of money. Therefore, it is a good idea to set a definite amount of money we want to attract into our lives.

It is also better that we always pay ourselves first and then our creditors. This behaviour will send a clear signal to our own unconscious mind and the entire universe that we always come first and we deserve to be wealthy.

Another important thought is that we should not let people owe us money, although, of course, we can and should be charitable. Having others in our debt means we repel money. If we don't get paid back, then what is the message we are sending to our unconscious? We want people who owe us money to like us; but they don't, because they feel guilty about not paying their debts and they tend to associate those feelings with us. There is a well-known rhyme, 'Never borrow never lend, if you want to keep a friend'. (Of course, here, we are referring to lending money on a personal basis. Clearly, money being borrowed or lent on a commercial basis, such as a mortgage or business loan, is an entirely different matter.)

We have already said we should be positive about money, but we also need to remember, many so-called successful people are very unhappy in their personal lives. They let money rule their lives. Money must always remain our servant. So when deciding what personal success should be, making more money is part of the way we achieve success, but nothing more. True happiness cannot be found by merely making money.

Remember!

The first step to make wealth flow into our life is to change our thoughts and attitude toward the idea of making money. Clear our mind of any negative concepts of wealth. This is done by bringing carefully analysing all of our thoughts and ideas about wealth, money and prosperity.

We have to take time to decide exactly what 'success' means to us. Is it earning a lot of money?

Are we a product of our circumstances? Has the path our life has taken been determined largely by forces beyond our control? Even if this is the case, stop believing it. Persuade ourselves that we're in control or fully responsible for our own life.

Taking responsibility for our life will empower us, foster success, and heighten self-esteem, all of which will lead to increased happiness.

Accept responsibility for who we are, who we will become, the choices we make, and the consequences that will result.

All confident persons accept that mistakes are inevitable. When they occur, they know how to handle them. That's what having a confident attitude is all about. With that positive outlook they put themselves in the very best mental state to master any new challenge.

Our thoughts and feelings must both consciously and unconsciously support the belief that we easily attract money. Our attitude to money has been set since we were a small child. Change this by adopting wealthy ways of thinking.

To run our own business, we need a set of targets, a detailed plan to achieve in order to achieve them and a genuine sense of inspiration. Find a business that expresses our true purpose or passion in life.

Get rid of any beliefs which make us think we cannot be wealthy. Open up our mind. Search for answers, unwrap possibilities, experience the excitement of the moment, perfect our dreams.

Just as we can from small seeds, grow crops, we can start a business or vocation with an idea. Nurture it by feeling inspired, have faith, believe in ourselves, focus on the present, use our imagination and eventually we will reap financial success.

Wealth is not restricted only to money and possessions. It manifests itself in many ways. A person can be wealthy with love, compassion, goodness, strength, energy, knowledge and wisdom.

Remember the three MUSTS to financial success – live upon less than we could earn – take advice from those who are competent and – have a plan to save regularly, perhaps 10% of our net income. This will accumulate over a long period.

We ought to make the firm decision to be rich, listen to and act upon what our unconscious tell us. Action, a simple act of doing something, stimulates our emotions and then we feel motivated to carry on.

PART SIX

Other essential routes to success

21
The Power of Prayer

The Power of Prayer and Meditation

The word *prayer* comes from the Latin *precari*, meaning *to request* or *to entreat*. Its current meaning is *to speak to God in order to give thanks or to request something*.

> 'If the only prayer you said was 'thank you' that would be enough.' – Meister Eckhart, philosopher and mystic.

There is help; all we have to do is ask! Prayer isn't just saying words; prayer is talking to God directly. How wonderful this is! Prayer is a great privilege, not something forced on us.

Some of us are afraid to pray for success because we can't believe God will grant it. If we don't ask, we will receive nothing. Prayer doesn't work through doubt. To God, doubt is like a foreign language, as it would be to us all. When we pray, we must believe that God hears every word we speak. He promises to hear us and He does hear us, for God has told us this and He cannot lie. That is why prayer is such a powerful force. We underestimate its power. Prayer can move mountains. Because of the power of prayer, we should never feel hopeless. Prayer changes things, specifically for the person who prays.

> 'I know that when I pray, something wonderful happens. Not just to the person or persons for whom I'm praying, but also something wonderful happens to me. I'm grateful that I'm heard.' – Maya Angelou, author, poet, actress.

Prayers are answered when our unconscious mind responds to the mental picture of thought in our conscious mind. One of the laws of life is that belief is a thought in our mind and that every desire is a prayer. An answered prayer is the realisation of the heart's desire.

Part of the language of prayer is the emotional state we experience as we pray. Our Creator can listen even to our silent prayers. The best way to pray is not through the repetition of words, but through the generation of truest feelings.

Meditation

Every time we concentrate on something for more than a few seconds we are indeed meditating. *Meditation* comes from the Latin root '*med*' meaning 'to measure' – the same root as the word *medicine*. Meditation is one of the best medicines available. It is a great way to escape the grind of daily life and has both mental and physical benefits. This includes reducing stress, lowering blood pressure, and is truly comforting. It can even boost our immune system!

Exercise one:
* Identify your goals. Define the changes you wish to make to your life
* Write them down on a sheet of paper. It definitely helps to do so
* Don't get hung up on the word 'meditation.' We're not talking about specific forms of Eastern or religious meditation. We're simply entering into the theta state as explained in Chapter 5 where we can connect to our unconscious
* The next stage is to pick a time when you will be uninterrupted for 10 to 15 minutes
* Focus on and visualise your desires at this moment

The best time to do this is in the morning when we've just woken up or at night just before going to bed. As our thoughts, expectations and joy are released during the day, they will become physically manifested through the universe.

At night, asleep, because of our dreams our inner self becomes more active.

The inner self doesn't need to rest. It is taking care of anything it may need or want including our desires. As we have handed over our desires or problems to the unconscious, our physical self is recuperating. We go to sleep contemplating our life's desires, joyfully awaiting the future. This exercise is very effective in making our dreams come true.

Exercise two:
- Find somewhere comfortable to sit so that you can relax, but that you don't fall asleep
- You do not have to worry about 'clearing your mind' or copying any other well-known meditation techniques, such as sitting cross-legged. Simply enter into the theta state while focusing on certain words or images linked to your desires
- Just spend 10 to 15 minutes daily performing this exercise

A person who regularly meditates is like a tree planted by the stream of water that remains evergreen. Everything s/he does will be successful. Meditation also helps us to improve our comprehension skills and memory. When we meditate, it strengthens our knowledge of what we've already learnt. As a carpenter transforms wood into a beautiful artifact, so mediation enables us to assemble facts into a logical pattern.

Indeed many who practise this process swear that it is the most productive 15 minutes of their entire day.

Remember!

Our prayers are answered when our unconscious mind responds to the images of our desires created in our conscious mind.

Do not pray for an easy life, pray to be stronger.

Prayer doesn't work through doubt.

Meditation is one of the best possible medicines.

22
The Right Friends

'A friend is a gift you give yourself.' – R.L. Stevenson, novelist and poet.

We should admire those better qualities we find in ourselves and in our friends and acquaintances. The people we choose to surround ourselves can be an inspiration, leading us to new exciting opportunities, or they can make us doubt ourselves and so inevitably we fail.

By combining our talents through positive teamwork, together we can achieve for more than any individual working alone. This approach is called synergy.

'Never doubt that a small group of thoughtful citizens can change the world. Indeed, it is the only thing that ever has.' – Margaret Mead, author and speaker.

Being encouraged is a basic human need. Without it, no one can thrive or even survive. That's why we should always hug our loved ones, or pat our friends on the back, both literally and figuratively. Indeed, good friends are like stars. We don't always see them but we know they're always there, ready to help us when needed. As well, it's better to hang out with people who have been more successful than us.

'Pick out associates whose behaviour is better than yours and you'll drift in that direction.' – Warren Buffett, business magnate and philanthropist.

Our circumstances need to be positive as well. This means surrounding ourselves with positive people, who love and believe in us and wish us to do well. Therefore, at the same time, it is always better to avoid those who are negative and jealous. **Our four closest friends influence us hugely.**

> 'You cannot expect to live a positive life if you hang with negative people.' – Joel Osteen, author and preacher.

If so far in life we haven't been successful we should find new associates. Being acquainted with **wealthy people** gives us the right mind-set. We start thinking like them. We extract the secrets of their success from their unconscious mind. As the author, Napoleon Hill, puts it in *The Master Mind Alliance*, 'Our friends should be our allies, chosen for their abilities to help us succeed.'

On the other hand, we shouldn't be necessarily scared of our enemies. After all it may well mean we are on the side of angels.

> 'You have enemies? Good. It means you have stood for something in your life.' – Winston Churchill.

At the same time, whenever it is possible, genuinely strive for a mutually beneficial solution to any disagreement. To value and respect people by understanding what and who they are is the best kind of victory for this means that everyone can feel they've benefitted, rather than simply one person gaining the upper hand.

> 'Keep away from people who belittle your ambitions. Small people always do that, but the really great make you feel that you, too, can be great.' – Mark Twain, author and humourist.

By being a sympathetic listener, trying to understand the other person's point of view means you will also find a ready response to your ideas. This helps to solve problems far more easily.

Once again it is emphasised that our choice of mentor is always vital. To help you make the right choice, it's a good idea to picture a decent, friendly, straight-talking friend. Then we can ask ourselves, whether this is someone we already know or would like to know? Asking others whom they would choose as a mentor is another sensible approach.

However, self-analysis is also important. This can be a way of improving self-confidence as well.

That's why we need to find out what other successful people advise. Reading around your chosen subject is, self-evidently, also an important and necessary step forward.

Remember!

Combining our different strengths through positive teamwork means we can achieve far more than the lone individual. This is called synergy.

We all know already that knowledge is power but when we share our collective knowledge for a common purpose, seemingly insuperable barriers can be overcome.

Keep the company of positive people, who love and believe in us and in our potential.

23

Beyond Education – the University of Life

Education means more than acquiring knowledge. The real aim of education must be to develop intellect and character.

By improving education standards the whole of society benefits, as well as the individual, in areas such as health, parenting and crime prevention.

Education empowers. It is the most fundamental precondition for democracy and social justice. We see this every day all over the world. For example, improving education standards ultimately resulted in the Arab Spring. The people were able to understand at long last they were entitled to fair and honest government. (Unfortunately, apart from Tunisia, at the time of my writing this book, in the other countries affected by this development, the situation remains uncertain and unstable.)

Indeed, without education, there can be no successful social, economic or political development. This has been recognised by the world community. The Second Millennium Development Goal, as specified by the United Nations, states that everyone should have access to basic education as a fundamental human right. There has been progress, although it has been slow and varies greatly from region to region.

As global competition increases, the necessity for educational improvement will only grow as the learning outcomes in the schools of our competitors keep on rising. The lightning-fast development of the Chinese economy suggests that their education system has radically improved. At the same time, there must be a real hunger for education among the young Chinese. Indeed, nearly every Chinese citizen under the age of 25 sees education as a key issue. It defines their lives.

Fundamentally, in this country, the present educational system gives our young children an external, objective and intellect-based education. However, it is mostly information that is rarely unified as knowledge.

'Knowledge advances not by repeating known facts, but by refuting false dogmas' – Karl Popper, professor of philosophy.

Despite of all the computers and interactive whiteboards, children spend years in an antiquated educational system. All too often, they are merely expected to regurgitate facts, rather than gaining the necessary skills to apply knowledge independently. For example, when studying foreign languages, they can pass their GCSE simply by memorising set phrases. This means they cannot form original sentences in the target language. This type of approach to learning leaves them ill-equipped for the modern world.

At the same time, schools fail to focus sufficiently on financial skills. Education is the foundation of success, but so is financial knowledge. However, we live in challenging times.

'One of the reasons the rich get richer, the poor get poorer, and the middle class struggles in debt is because the subject of money is taught at home, not in school. The rich teach their children differently. They teach their children at home, around the dinner table. What can a poor parent tell their child about money? They simply say "Stay in school and study hard." The child may graduate with excellent grades but with a poor person's financial programming and mind-set.' – Robert Kiyosaki, self-help author, motivational speaker.

In addition, exam success does not automatically lead to a high-paying job with great benefits, nor does it prepare the young for the real world. Therefore, a more sophisticated system of education is needed.

The present system is too much of a conveyor belt; it moves all children along, regardless of ability at a certain pace, too fast for most, too slow for many. It is unacceptable that a third of children fail to achieve expected levels of core knowledge and skills. Given the deliberate manipulation of official data, permitted through the connivance of politicians, exam grades improve while in reality academic standards fall. We must have instead a far clearer and much more consistent unit of measurement as regards academic achievement. Only then, can we truly judge both the success of individual schools and the system itself. This should also include a transparent analysis of how well young people develop and mature. For example, as Kate Reardon, author and journalist has written, 'A good school teaches you resilience – that ability to bounce back.'

Each second we live is a new and unique moment of the universe, a moment that will never be again and what do we teach our children? We teach them that two and two make four and that London is the capital of the UK. When will we also teach them what they are? We are taught to compete, to become like others and never be appreciated for **who we really are.** In other words, we are never taught that each one of us has our own unique gifts.

In short, the present type of school system prepares the future generation, as was done in the past, to have just about enough skills to earn a living. Into the bargain, many of our young people have become far too materialistic, not realising their goal in life is to worship a falsehood.

On a more positive note, achieving great success today is no longer mostly determined by the colour of skin, our country of origin, or even our individual parents, although social origins still play a considerable role in academic success or failure. As we mentioned in Chapter 17, positive role models are vital for personal success. Competition between schools means the children of successful professionals coalesce in middle class schools, the working class in working class schools. Unfortunately, therefore, the working class child, regardless of his/her ability, encounters far too few examples of professional success among the families of his/her pears. Consequently, there is no one in their daily lives who can raise the aspirations of these children and make them want to fulfil their true potential.

A fundamental rebalancing of the world economy is already underway and the global workforce is growing rapidly. Businesses are becoming much more international. Improved education inclusive of financial and communication skills also brings other important benefits. The purpose of education cannot only be economic. Inspiring ambition, aspiration and resilience in young people drives economic performance, of course, but it also predicts wider civic engagement and an ability to cope with modern life – CBI: 'Better education should be our overriding long-term priority'.

Unfortunately, mankind does not seem to have realised the basic social obligations – in essence caring for and respecting one another – that come with life on this planet. These can only be fulfilled if, along with an academic education, children also experience internal, subjective and intuition-based education as well. The latter requires the child to get to know himself/herself a bit more intimately. Although we are advised to socialise with our friends and relatives, rarely does one get to realise how pleasant and important it is to socialise with oneself once in a while!

> 'This is an attempt to initiate the young child into the inner world of man where wisdom dwells. The inner universal wisdom has to be brought to the surface to be used for one's own good and for the good of society. When the child gets to know that it has come from the same source from where all life has originally emanated, the child would get to realise the need to live in harmony with others, as also with Mother Nature. This, in addition, would make the child humble, humility being the core of real education.' – Professor B. M. Hegde, medical scientist, educationist and author.

Every action has an equal and opposite reaction, which means to live wisely is to live compassionately. If this were true of all of us, so many horrors in this world would never happen.

> 'Education without values, as useful as it is, seems rather to make man a more clever devil.' – C.S. Lewis, novelist, poet and academic.

This is my humble contribution to the education debate. There are those who think that there is nothing wrong with the present system as all of us are its product. They are wrong!

Remember!

Without being educated, no one can succeed. Being properly educated means you have learnt to cope with new challenges.

Learn how to think, not what to think. This opens the door to new opportunities and allows us to succeed to a far greater degree.

One key factor that determines financial success nowadays is the kind of choice we make.

The present educational system does not cater properly for monetary and communication skills, without which it is impossible to prosper.

Find out who you really are. Identify and exploit your own unique gifts and skills.

We also need an intuition-based system of education. This will enable us to bring to the surface the inner universal wisdom which can be used for our own good and for the good of society.

Always aspire.

www.ingramcontent.com/pod-product-compliance
Lightning Source LLC
LaVergne TN
LVHW041221080426
835508LV00011B/1028